Part I. *Une passion Chinoise*

Part II. Chasing butterfly: Confessions of a murderer

Part I. *Une passion Chinoise*

Butterfly

A novel

by Julie O'Yang

"'Butterfly is a tour de force...James Joyce of the Orient."

Leanne Delehanty, author and visual artist

"A passionate piece of prose full of unexpected wonderment"

Ma Jian, author of Beijing Coma

"...this is nothing like I've read before. The writing style is "different", somewhat a la Haruki Murakami."

The Vault of Books

"...one book I really enjoyed...a mesmerising literary work which melds fantasy with reality and past with present, to weave a story of love and forgiveness...with powerful and original imagery."

Dionne Lister, Australian writer

"...Scratching, tearing. We tear with it as it tears at us -- wounding, destroying even, but never devastating, for amidst everything there is laughter." Jeremy Fernado, author of various publications.

He works in the intersections of literature, philosophy, and the media and is Jean Baudrillard Fellow at The European Graduate School.

"Highly recommended!" Bibliography Masters, Brooklyn, NYC

"[Butterfly] has all the essential ingredients that makes a bestseller. There never seems to be a damp moment with the right choice of words. The book moves at a smooth pace throughout, and ends beautifully on the bank of the Yangtze River." Creative Ecstasy

There were hints of sunrise on the rim of the sky, yet it was still dark, and the traces of morning color were like goldfish swimming in ink.

Truman Capote, The Muses Are Heard

Time to gather lotus in the Yangtze Valley,
As lotus leaves are fair and lusty.
Fish frolic amidst the lotus leaves.
Fish frolic to the east of the lotus leaves,
Fish frolic to the west of the lotus leaves,
Fish frolic to the south of the lotus leaves,
Fish frolic to the north of the lotus leaves.

A *Yuefu* poem from Han dynasty (206 BC-220 AD)

Life,
Love,
our Country,
our Liberty.

Dedicated to a past and a future

My thanks go to everything under heaven, to my parents who bear with me, to P & D, "a nation of three", to all my (non-) virtual friends for your love. And thank you, Robert Masterson for your generosity with your time and your friendship.

Dr. Reigan walks down the corridor that smells of antiseptics. *The odour of death.* He prefers it more to the bottles of scents Alice lined up this morning on the breakfast table. "We are taking this into production. I need your opinion," she said pushing the unscrewed flasks over in front of his rice porridge. Little spheres of white porcelain. Curved zeros, lonely. Alice pushed them one by one with her long fingers, trimmed, deep scarlet nail polish. "What was the name of this one again?" he asked while taking a guarded sniff from the bottled fragrance concocted by his wife. "*La mémoire,*" the scent composer answered in dreamy tones. "Shush!" she added quickly in thrilled undertone, her cheeks rosy. She looked like a doll. "Perfume is like happiness. As soon as you try to explain the magic it's gone," said the doll with beautiful long fingers and scarlet nail polish.

True, you can't argue with the science of scent just as one cannot cancel out the question of life, Dr. Reigan ponders. In fact with this whole bolded capitalised Q, the quiz still kills him every single day, and there are nights that it really gets to him. Him, a human male in his early thirties, already a veteran in this work, walking down the passage that smells of death in his bouncy, quiet paces right at this moment. Like in real life, the journey through the hospital can be tragic, painful or sometimes just plain funny, although the professional protocols do not allow virus-related humour like computers; as a medical doctor you aren't supposed to be bored with your patients. The distance of no more than a hundred metres which he walks daily – he knows every inch of it, every detail is as he imagines it could be – but which would transport him beyond these grey walls to alight on an eternal path paved with childhood dreams and flying machines! He *feels* happy. Perhaps this was why he opted to study medicine many years ago, although his father rather saw him becoming an architect, Reigan recalls. As a child he showed a gift in drawing, and his father had a fascination for ancient Roman concrete buildings.

"They hold the spirits of people who once lived in them. Buildings don't rot away like human flesh. Concrete lasts; love does not. Love is a star in dark sky: in the end all stars DIE."

His father's words. He died last summer; Reigan hadn't had the chance to prove he was wrong about love.

Concrete.

Reigan repeats the word voiceless as he walks down the cement corridor. Darkness, coldness, and cruelty. Just like our existence, but nothing more. He wonders why such material was ever created, except that you could find in there some proof badly needed for this evanescent, day-to-day life, a metaphor perhaps, in an attempt to hold onto that which you believe is the hard copy of reality. Polished concrete, decorative concrete, concrete lace. He recalls the ad he sees every morning along the highway to work. "Build something great. Luminex Concrete is your triumph over life's threats and calamities."

Concrete. Concresco. Com, together. Cresco, to grow. Latin. Memory made of rubble, that was the secret of Pantheon, a temple for the illustrious dead honoured for the wars they fought. War, the undying temptation. War. And love.

War is concrete matter, solid with certain components, love by contrast is but a delicate, elusive song we sing. So Dr. Reigan thinks while meandering his way to the morgue.

Corridor, then another corridor, parallel, like two luminous lines taken from an haiku, with the interval of the lift. This afternoon he has to check on a case of brain death. It came a bit out of the blue, but it does happen, and Reigan said he would. After all, he is in charge of the neurological department of the hospital.

He remembers the day he got the job.

"We could use some young daring brains. I believe it's time for us to make our dreams come true. Give it your best shot and make us famous, Dr. Reigan!" the hospital director said at his job interview. He said he had read Reigan's article in the renowned medical quarterly: "Most *intriguing*." When he was up and started walking towards the door, Reigan heard the deep, clear trombone voice speaking behind him.

"One more thing…"

Reigan halted and spun around, more sharply than he had intended.

"Please, sir?"

"Oh nothing. I was just thinking…Your name, young man. Doesn't it mean something like "magic remedy"? If I'm not mistaken, *Rei* stands for the mind or magic – yes, only in a language like ours you can say two things using the same ideogram, from which I could but draw one conclusion: our mind is magic, and *Gan* suggests a small, medicated candy. You are meant to be a champion, I imagine!"

Yeah, well, what's in a name, Reigan remembers he thought at that moment, since he knew his new boss' family name was Lai. Lai is like a Pandora's box full of goodie gifts from a hug to a lazy dragon. But it can also mean an illness and has a hint of "eczema" in it. Dr. Lai studied dermatology in his younger days. He treated the "treeman", one of the most peculiar cases of skin disease ever recorded in medical history. The patient grew gnarled, root-like extensions on his limbs, so many of them that in the end he looked like a tormented Were-Willow!

Five years have passed since that job interview. War and love. Love and war. Reigan has seen plenty of the odd pair in action over the years as he contended with the jealousy of his peers, managed blade-to-blade combat for every attack on his irregular approach towards each individual case. He found the one thing the world is consequent about is its tight-fisted kindness. Therefore, love seems an alien creature from outer space.

"*Hello!* My name is Romeo. I'm green, I'm from Mars. We come in peace – shoot to love! Dr. Tender Warrior, you are brilliant! You are a GENIUS!" His wife Alice would poke fun at him for being a dreamy egghead. All's fair in love and war. In time, the neurological research centre Reigan leads has risen to be one of the most influential institutes in the field. He won his war. Now people say: I knew it. They say it in a way as if he owed that to THEM.

Reigan pushes the button. The lift starts with a jolt, and soundlessly descending like a cold snowflake into the "blind world", one of Dante's quizzes packed with metrical queen bees and lusty lover. The world runs on guilt and pains plus some medicine.

He clenches one icy fist as the lift halts. The door opens with a smooth shuffle. He steps out into the desolate, grim space. The door behind him shuts. Drawing a deep breath, he resumes his unperturbed pace towards the heavy metal door at the far end of this particular corridor. Overhead a moth thrashes about an electric light tube flickering on and off. Except for the pinging sound and delicate beating wings that are the only sign of life, the entire floor is so deadly quiet that it feels like a subterranean vault, even the air has that curious, sterilised reek of eternity. "It's the smell of Afraidium, son," his father once explained fear to him when he was little. "It's yellow and tastes like chicken."

Reigan hesitates a second. Reaching out to type the access code, his other hand floats to turn the stainless steel handle. A quick blast of frigid, icy air slinking across from deep inside, caressing his cheeks. He swallows, a sensation in his belly like a tickling, sharp talon. Princess Barefoot is not taking her day off from duties. He is struck by a wave of anxiety he knew ever since he was a child when encountered with the unfamiliar. The effect of death never seems to wear out. Even in the morgue of a hospital, death put under clean, white sheets, death fixed in ice cells, it's the old death brand new each time. Awkward. Foreign. Like death.

Clearing his throat, he approaches the stretcher cart. He pulls the sheet with one quick tug. Starched quality cotton, rustling. The woman's face shows. Very normal. So normal as if nothing had happened, and she would sit up at any moment and smile to him and tell him that she is happy, and that the answer is one single word; the four letter word we all try to find in our lives, with the little magic fishing rod "l" in the front – and sometimes, quite sometimes, it's burning. The essence of life has fled her nostrils like a trail of smoke drifting into the darkness, mesmeric and shiny. *Like a goldfish*, Reigan whispers.

Normality bothers Reigan every time he visits the morgue. He expects drama where there is none. Waiting for him is only the silence; loss doesn't have much to say. All the bickering and algebra and tragic and suicidal film stars you either like or dislike, every bit of self-importance seems pointless. Death doesn't make one feel proud. In his department, though, loss is ever active and noisy, giving him the illusion that he could help. Help those who have lost the vital part of life: the mind. And Reigan *wants* to help. He recalls the day when he came down here to check on his dead father. For a moment he caught himself expecting a miracle, that his father would suddenly split open his eyes and speak in his good-natured but stern voice: "We can't afford to make mistakes, can we, my boy?" He wants hope where there is none. Hope. His drug.

Reigan points the thin pillar of penlight into one eyelid. The woman feels supple and soft, her body must have been brought in a minute ago. He examines her other eye. Pulling back the sheet to re-cover, his hand stops in midair. He stares at the stranger's face. Big lashes skirting the delicate, china-like eyeshells, a vivid mouth, and a pert nose which he can't resist to touch. He lays a finger to the perfect arch, a touch so brief as if only to tap air. He never knew death could be so sensual and tender. All of a sudden he feels like crying –

But then, Reigan shivers. At first he thinks it was the arctic climate. He thinks he hallucinated, like the madmen he deals with daily. Schizophrenics who speak in word salad to warn him of the dead who are not dead, to caution him in low sound that Chairman Mao has returned to earth with horns and wings. Back home, Reigan tried to catch the image on Xuan paper. He had never thought of the Chairman in that quirky sort of way. In the margin of the grainy paper he wrote *Black angel*, like an ancient Chinese painting. Alice said it was his best artwork yet. She said tattered minds are original because they don't care they are ridiculous. She said she wanted to add the black angel to her upcoming autumn/winter line of fragrance and clothes. "Shakespearean" is the word Alice uses to define her midnight sweetheart chic made of ripped black satin and laces. Breezy laces, as if one is watching a dash of black ink taking flight in clear water. " 'Give me my robe, put on my crown, I have immortal longings in me,' " she recited the other night in a loud and clear voice when Reigan came home from late shift to find her atop the blue velvet couch, naked from head to foot waiting for him. The impish queen threw back her curly, dazzling head, a series of short-breathed laughs made her breasts flutter like young birds. She seduced him, and he let himself be seduced. Reigan remembers he fell in love first with the laugh of the woman, then the woman. Love is like fishing, and you throw out your heart as bait –

...immortal longings... Of the dead. Of the living.

Reigan shivers. The light overhead trembles, and dims. He makes sure this is not some neurological trick. In front of him the white wall is slowly drenched in a vile liquid. He gawps at the bleeding hollow. From the overflowing, aqueous grave, small and large drops of cinnabar seep out, thick strings of blood pearls trickling down, washing off a freshly painted lotus field like a hellish summer shower. Hissings of a huge white-hot iron bar pressing through a warp in time, the purest red, shot with torrid tar gold. Reigan listens to the faintest sound. Then, with a shudder, he realises it is a whispering voice. An evil corpse that jaws and swears just like in bad horror movies. *We are here to work; we don't run away,* he tries to convince himself. Riveted to the spot with terror, he keeps his eyes fixed on the wall losing so much blood volume. Black, scarlet pools gather around his feet, the smell of it makes him feel a little light-headed. Through the wobbly sound of murmurs, a giant pale expression reveals; a grin without a cat, vanishing into a blindingly radiant light. Somewhere, something stirred. Somewhere, something incredible is waiting to be known. From the bottom of black invisible water, Rorschach ink blots start to float to the surface of the large bare wall. Gaudy wings arise, gently unfurling from an indefinite glowing stupor, squirming and twisted, charred by their own intensity. A ghostly apparition thaws out to fill up the edges with new shades of phosphorescent and inky blue and green. Then, like an imploding star, the grisly, spangled shadow condenses to dotting zero. In the vacant field of a memory, Reigan discerns a familiar shape surfacing, shiny and mesmeric. *Death, like a goldfish. Or a goldfish, like death.*

The overhead light tubes brightens again. Rushing to the entrance, Reigan moves towards the adjacent room hidden in the gloom. The black fat padlock emerges, winking at him. Rusty iron, like blushing shame. With beads of moisture upon his white face, he hurriedly presses his ear against the wall oozing the last drops of liquid light. "Help me…" The voice fades in a frothy sound thick with swarms of air rising from the faltering, feeble lips. Somebody is drowning inside these corridor walls! Completely bewildered, his eyes pursue the strange orange halo swelling under his feet, his hands seeking to break the large butterfly twist latch on the sealed door. Reigan never bothered to ask why this sickroom was forever kept empty and locked. *"Funny,"* he had merely thought. In fact this wouldn't annoy him if something hadn't happened this summer.

Every year death rates spike during the torturous Dog Days. Elderly persons especially don't survive The Furnace – Nanking's nickname for the season – or The Inferno – Alice's brand name for Shanghai. The densely populated region of well over 20 million inhabitants depends on the service of one

A curious fish stall

public hospital. However, after the critical term passed peacefully, an Indian summer phased in at once. Like the lingering ghost of a dead lover that wishes to clear up an old debt, for weeks the heat wave kept on, refusing its delayed leave. Within a month, the hospital is flooded by people of all age groups, debilitating migraine is the most significant shared symptom. As the mysterious epidemic flare across the metropolitan area, identical nervous disorders manifest on all victims without exception. Patients suffer from acute nausea, including heavy, foamy vomiting similar to epileptic seizures. A nine-year-old girl repeatedly banged her head during an attack. Unspeakably terrified of light, the child shouted and cried in a shrill, piercing voice. She insisted that she saw a malicious, winged creature swimming around her fairy nightlight, luring her with most appalling gestures. She screamed her head off in sheer, unadulterated panic before passing out for 24 hours. During the night observation, Reigan listened to her jumbled grunts as if the little girl was possessed by a slighted banshee speaking with her sugar sweet tongue – which stupefied the doctor.

Suddenly, and without intent, his mind floats to the fisherman from the Yangtze.

On Friday on his way home, Reigan would stop at the fisherman's shop for a couple of loaches from the river Yangtze. "Brew a wonderful soup with tofu for your wife. She will be pregnant soon!" The fisherman has the most curious stall he has ever seen. In the fan-shape front of painted red latticework, a square is cut out for the fishes, alive and jumping, to be handed to clients. Every time Reigan feels he is peering into the old days, into an ancient painting he has grown part of, and that – Reigan has discovered – is how the fisherman keeps his fare fresh. "You ever saw food go bad on an ink painting, doctor?"

…immortal longings… Of the dead. Of the living

"Returning to earth is not the black angel but something more harmful and dangerous," the fisherman from the Yangtze proclaimed, raising an index finger covered with scales. "It is the return of the butterfly fish! This time, no-one is safe," the old man wheezed inexplicably.

"*The butterfly fish?*" Reigan heard himself repeat in a quiet but darker tone.

The fisherman narrowed his eyes on him, a crack running from ear to ear on the parched, lined face as if he had brought some euphoric news to all mankind. Reigan found himself at a loss for words: Fear was one of the things he learned as a child.

"*Wo shi ai.*" **My name is LOVE: forgive me!**

Trapped inside the grieving silence, the reedy, flitting voice speaks again. Reigan gawks at the halo, outstretched, unfolding its liquefying fringes, and mounting. A lucid shape rises to its breathtaking, final symmetry, burnt into his retina. Two mesmeric satin wings clenched around a warped body and her slender throat: pure light, fire and water.

"Come in –

Good morning, Dr. Reigan! I was just thinking about you – "

Director Lai sits at the Gispen desk in a larky mood, a teacup clutched between two hands, steaming. Reigan has always wondered how the man does this. Somehow holding a burning hot teacup without a whimper is a skill lost to all younger generations. "You guys never knew suffering," his father used to say when he was in a clouded mood. "You guys don't know that people have to really suffer before they can risk doing what they love." Nowadays kids prefer chilled ice tea from BK, Have It Your Way®. Sooner or later holding a burning hot teacup will be a legend.

"I was just thinking about you, Dr. Reigan. Sit."

The director points to a chair across his desk.

"*Reigan*, please." Taking a seat, Reigan requests in his vivid, kindly voice. "You are my boss and I would like to learn from you."

"You know, Dr. Reigan. You are one of those people who have won my admiration over the years. You and I, we can fix our nation and our world together."

"You said you were thinking of me, boss?"

"It's something I read at breakfast. Usually I forget the stuff written in the newspaper. It's always the same old story about Mr. Hu has become the president and Yu Stin Ki died in a place I never knew existed. Truth usually is the same old story. Why do I care? But one sentence gets stuck in my head,

I keep asking myself to whom can I turn with my question. Then I thought of you."

"What is it you read?"

" 'The soul is like a diamond'. Six words, printed in black on white. You are the one who looks into the house of the soul every day, Dr. Reigan. Brains, muscles and tissues that are given significance by the bunches of garlands of nerves. You are an archaeologist of the heart. So answer me this. Have you ever found a diamond in there?"

"I'm still a poor man."

"No diamond? Are you sure?"

"None whatsoever. Nor glass or metal – if you are brought in "healthy", that is, and in one piece." Reigan raised both his hands to make air quotes.

"So why do they write such nonsense?"

"It is a wish I suppose. We want our soul to be like a diamond, shiny, robust, and forever, but instead the soul is dark, fickle, transitory and unreliable. The soul is more like…"

"A summer pond full of lotus flowers?"

"I beg your pardon?"

The director turns away in his swivel chair to face the window view overlooking the lotus pond painted fiery pink and red by the morning sun.

"I wonder why we need these pretty things everywhere we look. To hide something from our eyes I'd say, but what exactly?"

Blowing tea leaves around the teacup, he takes a silent, bird sip.

"One must take a deep dive to the bottom to explore the secrets. Treasures, lost charts, long-forgotten yarns, and ephemera. Only then he will know if it's only useless mud or there is something else – "

"Something else? Like what?"

The director doesn't speak for a while, silently looking out the window on a perfect day. Dragonflies dart in the cool of giant, inky leaves, dilly-dallying, their wings flushing flimsy. His back turned towards Reigan, suddenly he mutters in a low voice curiously highlighting every word.

"The. Truth," he says. "The. True. Splendour. Of. Our. Being."

The lotus pond existed long before the war. It's more like a resort where they work rather than a hospital – Reigan ponders – hidden in the lush greenery and breezy on hilltop during *autumn tiger* (Indian summer for the locals). Down the slope runs a brook that joins the Yangtze at one point. The big river, after skirting Shanghai, empties into the Pacific Ocean, carrying dirt and fatigue of the journey behind to finally become a sun-glazed shadow on the horizon.

When the first high-rise buildings rose among these hills – so Reigan was told by the eldest nurse of the hospital – it was 1948, one year before Chairman Mao proclaimed the founding of the People's Republic, the nurse was not yet fifteen. The engineer who drew up building plans kept the lotus pond. He didn't allow it to be closed off with cement. Because pretty flowers can inspire good Feng Shui, as she reasoned. For her, Feng Shui is looks plus a bit of Alice in Wonderland. In the years to come, people forgot all about flowers for nobody cared about anything except his own hungry belly in those days. However, the pond seemed to live another life on another planet. Like a crazed spirit, the lush field of flowers survived all those who perished during the nation's largest, most violent insanity exhibition that still makes people laugh and cry until this day.

"I'm sorry if I made you confused, young man." Spinning around in a semi-circle to face Reigan, the director speaks in his warm, metallic voice. "This is how I start my day, a little mental gymnastics is best cure for AD and the other old age disease. To let the fancy roam. Feel *free*. After that I can handle life –

What's up, champion? I see something is bothering you?"

Reigan tells. He deliberately left out the crucial part, only arguing that they will need extra sickrooms pretty soon because the Indian summer has taken its toll blah blah blah. Isn't he supposed to take care of those who hear what is not there to be heard, who build castles on stilts of fancy? They are called: patients. And they trust him, the kind of trust only an old blind cat would have for the world since there is not much choice left. But Dr. Reigan is seeing cobalt in the wall himself! To let the fancy roam, easy said, but whoever takes that kind of risk is either a moron or will win a Nobel Prize.

"I need the key," Reigan says in the end.

The director lets a few long seconds pass, fixedly watching him out of a pair of austere eyes.

"All right. I want to know what the hell is going on in there. You know me, boss. If I want to be in that room, I will be in that room."

The man doesn't move a muscle, silently studying Reigan with a fatherly expression, choosing his words with care.

"Knowing is prison. Are you sure you want to know, Dr. Reigan?"

"The answer is: YES."

Reigan clears his throat husky of heroism.

"Then sit tight, for I have a story to tell."

"During the Cultural Revolution, I was sent to work in the countryside together with many others. "Sending down" was the terminology. I was young in those days, and like you I wanted to do great things and change the world. I was sent down to Wuan.

"It's a small village not far from here. Sitting on the bend of the river, protected by its geography, Wuan stayed for a long time an unnoticed paradise. That's the place where I was going to reform my counter-revolutionary mind through labour for the next ten years. People thought I was lucky. Some colleagues went to the Gobi and other terrible places – not that the places were terrible, just we city boys and girls weren't made for that sort tough life. Many of them never returned home. Horrible stories. I suppose I was very lucky indeed. At any rate, I saw it for the first time in Wuan, the small fishing village on the curved shores of the Yangtze. In the beginning I thought it was an illness. Then I realised it was not. Not EXACTLY."

Bending to blow on the tea he holds with saintly demeanour – blow, and sip – he looks at Reigan through a parting veil of steam.

"Dr. Reigan, do you remember the treeman?" Chewing on a tealeaf caught between his teeth, he asks abruptly.

Reigan has studied the medical case files of the patient in detail, he knows the entire history. Back in the 1960s, Dr. Lai, at the start of his career, took on a rare medical case. "The man who grows roots on his limbs". Except, of course, they were not roots but extensive verruca growth. Warts mushroomed from a virus in the blood and grew little by little into lumps the size of small, burnt out pine stumps. Wild, raw shoots thriving on human flesh. In the end, after all the shavings and trimmings, there was no man left. He became his own Eliotesque jungle! However, newspapers at the time reported that the twenty-five-year Dr. Lai had probably found a way to track the virus. He had started developing a potential treatment for the patient tortured by severe physical pain. Meanwhile, the Cultural Revolution was in full swing. The "treeman" became the reason for Dr. Lai's future persecution. The hospital was disbanded. Doctors and nurses were sent home. The young skin specialist was sent down to work on land just so somebody like him could learn from the farmers how to fertilise rice paddies, castrate a cow and slaughter a pig, which were considered far more important tasks than finding a groundbreaking cure to save a human life. What a human life is worth is perhaps not a scientific issue. Human lives are worth less than a fly in this country. Flies can make noises as much as they like, when they like, the Chinese endure in silence. This is a nation that regards silence as the highest music!

"The other day I was in the archive to look for some old pictures. I thought he looked rather revolutionary. The Eco-mutant strikes back. Fashionable," Reigan tries to crack a joke. "He could play the Ent in a Lord of the Rings movie. Tagline: "Made-in-PRC", truthful, no lies, what a stupid joke!"

His boss doesn't laugh, looking past him at something invisible.

"I met her by accident. No, she was not a talking tree and didn't grow a beard. It's even better or worse. You decide after we finished our story. In the morning – it was one of those ordinary mornings – so, in the morning, I went to the water tap in the village to wash myself. As I was having so much fun brushing my teeth up and down and taking my time to enjoy the scenery of the Yangtze Valley at sunrise, I heard the swishing footsteps. In the corner of my eye I caught a shadow approaching. At first I didn't realise why she looked so glassy, she was chased behind by a whirlpool of purple and gold stars. She carried a pitcher in her hands, unglazed terracotta. That moment changed my life, mornings are never the same again!"

"Don't tell me she was the River Empress and asked you to marry her?"

"It was the Indian summer, she came for some water to have a shower behind the bushes. She walked past me – I'm not sure how to describe the way she moved herself. Amble? Swim? Skulk? I think it's skulking, you know, like a fire fox gambols about the looming shadows, the sort slinky, shrewd, cool treads. *I mean*, she walked like a fish if only they had legs. As if she felt my eyes on her, she swirled around and smiled at me. Then I saw her bared arms: they were *completely* covered in fish scales! I was STUNNED. I was speechless, thunderstruck by her magnificent beauty. It was absolutely a work of mad genius. She looked like the daughter of a mermaid who made love to a goldfish. An extraordinary picture, wonderfully weird, a statement I should have sympathised with during those dark years of our history. And yet this other man in me who never forgets to be a doctor said I should stop her and figure it out."

"Did you?"

"She told me that sometimes the symptoms would abate. But every month after the full moon, the patterns would grow back exactly the same way in exactly the same golden orange hue. Her skin was glowing, dense and cool to the touch, no unevenness at all, smooth as silk bejewelled with tightly packed little sequins, gold, pearly and precious slivers. Oh! Such gorgeousness, I didn't *want* it to be a fatal disease.

She told me she was not the only one, all the way down the river there were hundreds of them just like her. Some girls may have a patch of flaked skin hidden under her armpit or in other intimate places. But only they would know the truth."

"What's the truth?"

The director heaves a sigh and shakes his head in uncertainty.

"Hard to say. The truth is hardly ever pure but always simple. I must say that the story puzzled me back then. It still does today."

Looking briefly in his teacup, blowing but not drinking this time, he raises a pair of haunted eyes.

"Once upon a time there lived a young couple on the bending shore of the river Yangtze. The husband was a salt inspector, which means his job was commissioned by the emperor to control the quality of table salt. He was responsible for the distribution of good, safe salt. Every controlled ration must be given to every household in every small village along the long, long river, from tail to head. So all year round the husband had to travel, and every time he had to leave his bride behind.

"The young couple had been married for a while. On the wedding night they were delighted to find that they belonged to one another and were not meant to separate. But all year round the husband had to travel to do his job.

"Some journeys took longer than others. This time months passed. One evening at home, the wife felt lonely and sad. She cried for a long time in front of the house altar where Bodhisattva Guan Yin was venerated. After she had finished crying, she put the bowl filled with teardrops in front of Guan Yin's feet. The Goddess of Mercy of a Thousand Arms was very touched. She loves drop, drop, slow tears. It's her favourite sacrifice with which she will water her garden of most beautiful heart-shaped blossoms! 'If you wish, I will change you into a goldfish,' Bodhisattva Guan Yin spoke to the young wife, rising slowly from her gilded seat. 'You can swim after your husband's sampan every time he embarks on a journey. But I can do this only if you are certain. Are you certain?' The wife nodded YES. 'Then listen carefully,' the Goddess of Mercy went on, her countless arms brandishing in the gloom to form a formidable maze. 'In the hills near your house there is a lotus pond. On its edge there is a well. Drink from the water and you will change into a goldfish. It's important that you don't forget to take enough water from the well with you to catch up with your husband. When you have found him, drink the water you have brought and you will change from a fish into a beautiful woman. Then you can love your husband as much as you like. There is a price though for this pleasure. What is love worth without suffering and endurance?' said Bodhisattva Guan Yin in her calm, cruel, slightly weary voice, crisscrossing her limbs. In each of her hands she was holding a different charm. 'Because, young wife, every time you drink from the magic water, you will become another woman. Every time you visit your husband, you will witness his disloyalty. You will suffer. In the end, you will see that your man has forgotten all about you. There is another thing. You MUST swear this is a secret between you and me. If anyone, anyone at all ever comes to know of your change, you will stay a fish forever, and it's not my business to interfere with gods. I'm unable to give you back your human flesh. Do you consent?' The wife swore secrecy. 'There is no way back after I speak the incantation, do you understand?' Bodhisattva Guan Yin warned her for the last time. The wife understood. 'Well then, bid yourself farewell.'

"The Goddess of Mercy waved the lotus leaf expanding to become a gigantic umbrella concealing the most horrible secrets of the world. As white lightning flashed, accompanied by dull, rolling thunders, a vulnerable little creature materialised in the dark, with pretty, fanned fins. And so, the wife was to make acquaintance with all kinds of women, willowy or luscious, tall or tiny-footed, graceful lady or starry-eyed girl, a vast and encyclopaedic set of types. But never, ever was she to see herself again!"

"Whoa…" Reigan lets go a small sound.

"You are not convinced, Dr. Reigan. You don't believe that one could love so much that she is ready to give up being human."

"How's that?"

"Of all the tasks in the world, love is the most difficult. For one human being to love another is the ultimate; the last test and proof of our humanity. And most of us fail."

Reigan ponders for a minute.

"Carry on," he says.

"The wife became a goldfish. She went with her beloved husband on every voyage he undertook. She followed him as far as she could. She took risks in ferocious floods and the shallow mountain rills, said goodbye to monsoon and greeted icy Himalayan downpour. But at night, she would turn up at the inn where her husband stayed and make passionate love to him. Every time she was a different woman than the last."

"Did he know who they were? Did he find out that they were but one woman who loved him deeply?"

"No, he didn't. He made love to them, and he forgot about them just like he forgot her. But she did bear children for him."

"And she was a fish! She must have born him a spawn of offspring!"

"Hundreds of them, half fish half human."

"Mermaids?!"

"And they still walk around out there," the director affirms, nodding. "I saw many of them in the villages along the river during my clandestine investigative travels."

Reigan is flabbergasted, but not because of what he heard. There is a candid warmth in the voice, slightly mocking but magically spellbinding with its "hope & belief" youthfulness, a voice infused with a nostalgic ache that almost brought tears to his eyes. He remembers that his father spoke in the same way.

"That was what you saw yesterday in the morgue, didn't you? The light and everything?"

"You knew?!"

"Everybody knows but nobody speaks. Nobody asks why. 'Why?' is a question rarely asked in this country. I have been told that the light forebodes heartbreaks and misfortune. Last time people saw the orange shining under the door was in a night over forty years ago. I remember it clearly because the next day the Great Proletarian Cultural Revolution broke out officially in Beijing."

"I still don't see how these things connect – "

"Under that room there was once a well. *Exactly*. It's the same well whose water *cured* the wife and transformed her from fish to human. As time went by, finally the wife too forgot why she was doing all this. But she did remember what Bodhisattva Guan Yin said to her. One day, she went back to the well to drink water directly out of it. So – "

Arching his back, the director bends deeply to finish the last tea. He stares blankly into the emptied cup for some time, lost in thought.

"What happened next?" Reigan urges.

"In the water, she saw her past rolling and rolling in front of her eyes like a movie. She saw how it got started, what she looked like before the day of judgement. She remembered how she suffered over and over again, but yet she never gave up loving her husband. I think in the watery shadows she saw her soul, playing like a movie in front of her eye, more brilliant and amazing than Koh-I-Noor. By strange coincidence – or rather it was the tuning fork of order of things – I discovered that the village where I was sent to work was named after the well. Wuan: *forget me not.*"

"You have been to the room. *Haven't you? Why didn't* you tell me?"

"What is there to tell? That I'm losing it and I can join Dr. Reigan's Timmy Tammy Tommy in La Tofu Nutty Teahouse? No, thanks. I think I made other plans for life."

The man laughs shortly. "When you are young you are easily tempted. So to answer your question. Yes, I was tempted once."

"Did you find something?"

"Not much I'm afraid. A bed, one of the old-fashioned ones we had in the hospital, creaking like hell. White, clean sheets folded in a square as if waiting for the patient from long ago to return. I found some trails left haphazardly on the dusty floor, no human footprints, though. Have you ever seen loaches struggling for life on dry land before snapped up by a crane, Dr. Reigan? It's a beautiful spectacle, beautifully cruel. Well, there were these crimson gingery shiny little pieces all over the place. I came from a fisher's family, I scaled fish since I was four. I fancied fish skin as a child and collected scales of all kinds of strange fish washed ashore. From the thin round crystal plates I would make my own phantasmagoria lantern. But the strangest thing was the floor. It's not the common cement floor. Instead, it was entirely covered in mats."

"Mats?"

"Stone-grey tatami, large and comfortable, like from a trendy home magazine – I know, it is too good to be fiction."

"What else? Did you see more weird things?"

"That's all I believe. Oh, there *is* something. I don't remember why I took them. Perhaps for the sake of remembering now I come to think of it, like a souvenir – "

The man colours from embarrassment. Rising from his place, he walks to the cupboard. A grimy box appears with well-worn, old-style record sleeves lined up inside, tinted from a remote era. The box lands between them with a thud. Reigan leafs quickly through the old gramophone records. Smart covers with pretty girls in pretty clothes only seen on pretty pictures like these. The roaring night life of roaring clubs in roaring Shanghai in the Roaring Twenties.

"Jazz?"

"Music of the body. I think all doctors should listen to jazz. It reminds me of a healthy, strong heart pulsing in the night."

He is talking about the EKG, the electrocardiograph used to detect heart abnormalities and diseases.

The director turns to choose a dark pink sleeve from the box, inspiring shots of the old dust. He paces off to turn on the record player he has sitting on top of a shelf. A rasping female voice suddenly flows out to fill the gloomy space with a sundrenched song:

Summertime
And the livin' is easy
Fish are jumpin'

...

Pensively, Reigan stands up to leave. He feels even more puzzled than before he came, but completely hooked on the idea to get to the bottom of things. A phantasmagoria indeed. Which ghost is so picturesque and fantastic? His mind dwelling on the bizarre story, he walks down the long corridor past the curve when he hears the warm trombone voice rising behind him above the raspy tune from the ancient album:

"It's time you write medical history, *little bastard!*" Playfully mocking, fatherly.

...

So hush little baby

Knowing is prison.

Why the devil did he say that? Is this why millions of Chinese people choose to be silent, not because they are afraid to be put in jail. They are reluctant to stir the ghosts because of a confinement so dark and terrifying it would devastate one's mind. Silence is the best option. Silence is the best music, his father said and believed. Reigan didn't expect he would miss him so much. After the cremation, that evening he made love to Alice so violently it frightened him. Reigan realised something he hadn't before, that love is knowing you can lose.

He touches his finger to the aluminium key, tapping on the small pendant-size wet from sweat. He has been holding it in his hand since the morning. He holds it, puts it back on the same spot on his desk only to pick it up again to hold in his palm. He repeats the act almost unconsciously, with fetish accuracy as when he handles a diagnostic tool.

Knowing is prison.

"Put on a light for heaven's sake!"

Nurse Lyn walks in with a steaming cup in one hand, her other hand rubbing up and down the wall for a light switch.

"I brought you coffee, Dr. Reigan."

"Sorry, I forgot time passing while walking in the woods and finding some magic mushrooms and berries to pick. Mmmm. Heavenly mud, the slurpier the better."

His eyes batting from the sudden glare of electric light tubes, Reigan takes a big sip, running the hot liquid over his tongue. He hears a faint buzzing in his head. For hours he has been hiding in his office, browsing the Internet, searching for something, anything at all. There is not much information about Wuan, an indication that the fishing village is too small and unimportant. He did find an article about the Yangtze dolphins. Known as the "Guardian spirit of the Yangtze", the dolphins came to mate in the natural bay shaped at the big bend of river. However, the rare species living in the Yangtze river has allegedly become extinct over recent years. Google map shows the dappled, eye-shaped spot immediately adjacent to the drab oblong of the hospital building. Wuan is a village of probably no more than three hundred souls.

"It's ten o'clock. I'm off."

"Are you going somewhere?" Nurse Lyn is the new intern of his department. She is 22, the age of "anywhere but home".

"There is a dance party. I'm taking a taxi to the Bund to meet my girlfriend. See you tomorrow, Dr. Reigan."

The nurse turns to leave with a smile.

"Could you switch off the light please?" *In the dark I can think.*

"Thanks for coffee, Lyn! Kick up your heels!" Reigan calls after her, listening to her heels ticking pleasantly away on the off-white linoleum. The sleek red shine of leather dissolves all the way up to the bend in the corridor. The shoes remind him of the word "desire".

Stretching skywards then rubbing his eyes, he paces to the black hole of the window. Over the hills, the distant city flickering as if from another galaxy. Shanghai at night. Featureless brightness of a trillion lights. A trillion desires. Reigan once asked his buddy at the university – he was a student of Physics – whether it's possible to measure desire by linking to the amount of energy consumed by a community of people. New York's blackout in 1965 resulted in a baby boom nine months later, is that what you are talking about? asked the future physicist. Desire is birth-controlled, Reigan recalls he answered, because desire is so strong you can't afford the consequences.

A trillion desires of a trillion living souls. In the black sky no single star is to be seen. Suddenly the picture of his father rushes back to him. On bright summer evenings he would take little Reigan to the roof of their apartment block to watch stars extinguish and new ones being born. *Silence is the best music.* For many years father and son gazed into the immeasurable unknown without exchanging a word between them. It was at the time that Reigan knew his most brilliant ideas were born in these silent, brilliant hours, and that thoughts are like stars: he has to turn off the light to see them. Until one day father and son noticed that the stars were disappearing. They had counted a million answers and questions for many seasons together, now the diamonds switched off one by one in the ether of black velvet that brings you to your knees and drives you crazy with longings for itself. Light pollution, they said so on the news. Desire of mankind outshone that of gods.

A trillion desires of different lives. They suffer from insomnia, they are workaholic, they expect a nervous breakdown any moment, they are anal retentive, they have drug problems and constipations every morning. If your daily experiments of anodyne don't help, welcome to Shanghai where there is always a dance party.

Dr. Reigan tries to establish a diagnosis. Symptoms, context. Add up concern with parking space minus family disasters during last year's reunion. No cure. Except, perhaps, the little fishing rod will do the trick, the four letter magic word. The burning madness we can't live without and within.

The illness we die from and die from not having. The Empress of all maladies. The ghost –

A shadow rushing past him. A pair of night swallows shoots out from a hidden nest on the edge of the lotus pond, causing a sudden stir of inky, giant leaves in the sultry weather. *Shalalala*. My heart sings Shalalala. If knowing is prison and silence the best music, let's hear it. Blessed be EKG and fivefold *quantum sufficit*, let's do the almighty heartbeat.

Reigan marches back to his desk, picks up the aluminium key winking from the dark, tosses it in the air, and –

Catch!

The earthly air gives her a chill, sending a twirl up her slippery body, under her the wooden bed creaking. For Bodhisattva's sake, a fish doesn't belong on dry land, let alone a bed. She hears the voice in her head swear. What's she doing in a bed anyway? Waiting? For whom? Where is the water, the mud, the grass? A forest of sea grass would be fine now to hide her naked body.

She makes a vain effort to remember how she got here in this stuffy, little room of concrete walls and no window. Then, with a shock, she realises that she must have come here to *die*! This must be the Hell of the aquatic dominion. Since more than 70 per cent of the planet consists of water, she should expect the inferno prepared for her kind to be at least as tremendous and as grand. Instead it's a creaking everyday bed! This is the place where she will be slipping into the safe world of fantasy and awakening to reality, the place where she will better understand her very own self, her own feelings. If life can be compared to a journey, what gives value to travel is fear, and for one thing, life can teach us to be brave and loving. To love in spite of ourselves. The bed was the lovers' battlefield. This is where the lovers will be reunited after seventy years, in this bed, in this aqueous grave!

With the thought in mind, she shivers some more, reaching in the meanwhile for the folded white square of sheet at her feet. "They are not too ordinary, are they?" she hears herself saying without saying, looking to her feet, playing with her "pigeon toes". She examines two huge fans spread over the entire width of the bed's end. Huge fanned, webbed feet, black lace fringes satin. People call them tails or fins. She prefers to call them wings though. She often imagines herself to be a butterfly, always happy, always summer, her wings floating and whirling in the air like a secret wish.

The sheet opens out, throwing ripples of white waves over her entire body.

"I'm not exactly naked, am I?" she whispers to herself without whispering, looking quickly around to see if there is someone else present in the room. She doesn't consider herself a prudish person. But for fish nudity is a shroud!

She marvels at her torso smooth as glass, her foggy, haloed skin armoured in trimly patterned, rounded little blades of gold, silver and glittery ginger. Whether her gear is a disease or a choice by her own will she hasn't quite decided yet. The touch of luminosity astonishes her. The colour hasn't drained or turned pale over past decades. The oomphs stay on no matter how old she is. But she feels old and tired. Too old to remember how old and too tired to forget. Travelling alone may instill in oneself a sense of freedom she might otherwise not have possessed. This is the end, her date with fate will soon finish. Drawing the sheet to her chin with a slow, cautious move, she settles herself on the horrible, creaking bed, in a comfortable bearing, on her side, her back curled into a mirrored S.

"Dream," she thinks to herself without thinking. "Only in dreams harm will not meet you. Only in thoughts you don't dread the murmuring seas of silence, a terrible hurt that will lull you to sleep. *Embrace me*, pain and…tenderness."

Summer, 1944

"Come in, Wife. I was just thinking about you."

She hated to be called "Wife". He used to call her by her maiden name he was very fond of. Butterfly this and Butterfly that, Butterfly come to sit with me for a while, let's to bed, come, Butterfly. He was gentle, and she felt the luckiest woman in the world. Nothing was the same again as before, the past seemed a monochrome blur and she thought she would go crazy. Since the day six years ago, everything changed in their life.

"I was just thinking about you, Wife. Sit."

She took an uncertain step over the threshold, and stopped. Motionless, expressionless, she fixed her eyes on his face. And he understood her mind's voice. No love can survive muteness no matter how eloquent the silence is. After six years he had learned to understand her weeping muteness.

"Is there something you want to tell me, Wife?" he offered in an irritated voice, his eyes troubled. There was a time that his wife sang along to his favourite songs. People warned him of her and told him that she sang like a mermaid, the half-fish, half-woman monsters from the deep. They said a woman who lured a man like this wasn't a good sign – they proved to be right.

"Write it!" Inviting her in, he showed her a pile of old newspapers on the round tea table.

She took a few steps inside her husband's room, her hand touching purposely the sheet of calligraphy tucked in her breast pocket, showing the soot-black ink strokes written on rice paper for him to see. She wanted to annoy him. She wanted him to be angry with her, shout at her, slap her in her face, call her a whore. None of this happened, although he did look at her – at her breasts. She remembered that she once detested the strayed glance of men. It reminded her of the animal trapped in a human body, the animal in hers. Now she pined for that filthy, stealthy look because she knew it was her only chance to feel alive again. She had the firm, full breasts most Chinese women didn't – "my magnificent Himalayas", her husband called them – and she had a beauty spot in the left corner of her delightful mouth, not too high and not too low, not too big and not too small. An imperfection exactly right. She was made to be desired. But instead she felt dead. They were the living dead, buried alive by their own tragedy, on a sunny day six years ago.

She brushed past him. Taking a seat, she dipped a finger in the cup of tea that had gone cold and started writing on dusty newspaper spread in front of her across the tea table. A world without writing is such a burden to carry. Her husband had forbidden her to touch ink, rice paper and ink. Damn you, woman! If it had not been for you, your *art*! That was the last time he shouted at her, on the blackest day in the nation's history. Burning fire, screams of pain and terror. Hell on earth came without warning on one perfectly ordinary day. Ever since then he had abandoned her to the mercy of atonement in his own quest of trial. They were two hurt animals, wounded by the war which had brusquely, mercilessly entered their life in the hills fragrant from flowering herbs. Suddenly it was over before they knew what hit them, the sun, the fun, the cheers and laughter. Everything that glitters, everything effaced and washed away into the white water of the Yangtze. No herbal tea will warm them again and fill their chest with poetry and fine sentiment.

Sheng. She held up the only word she wrote, a name. Her eyes dry, her mouth distorted by endless fear and misery, she waited, watching his face slowly turn pale and turn red. At last she had succeeded to enrage him!

"*Sheng is dead!*" he hissed in a husky, mad voice. "Tears in heaven, the grass is singing on his grave, *if* he had one! Our son didn't wait to bury his father – "

Gasping, he yanked the newspaper out of her hand, so hard he tore it in half, knocking the tea sideways. The cold liquid wambled, the cup rolled and tripped over the edge, staining the calligraphy in her breast pocket with dark green and violet rings. Her eyes filled with dismal, tearless agony, she felt herself collapse to the floor trying to catch the broken pieces.

"Sheng is dead – Our son is dead – " His voice raised an octave higher as if to be certain of the meaning of the spoken words. It was too late.

"Calligraphy is the art of breathing, eh?" he continued shouting at her. "Let me tell you: the boy doesn't breathe anymore! YOU KILLED HIM. Did you forget?" The bellow lapsed into a toothless whimper.

She didn't forget. Today exactly six years ago.

In the morning she sent her son away with a scroll to bring to Mr. Lau, her regular client and patron. In fact, Sheng insisted that he wanted to go to Nanking alone. "To see a friend," he told his mother. The boy was to become eighteen after the moon feast.

"At his age the boy needs to have his own secrets," she had tried to persuade her husband to allow their son to travel. "He knew the city, he grew up there. If it hadn't been for the war we would still be living in Nanking."

Some months before her husband decided that the family should leave their home. The Japanese Imperial Army occupied the Northeast and quickly approached the Great Wall north of Beiping. In the major cities such as Shanghai and Nanking, tension increased dramatically within a matter of days, people were afraid. And although the authorities refused to give a clear picture of reality, the Chinese were prepared in expectation of armed soldiers marching into their lives, hailed by a cheering assembly of well-wishers and opportunists as happened in Manchuria. For them the war was obvious, politics anything but. Various newspapers on war and defence revealed little with their dull grey, gloomy looks to imitate realism and to hide the truth. Reality and truth are two fictitious characters in a novel who have nothing in common.

"Japanese or no Japanese, life for us should stay as ever," her husband had delivered his sermon. "We should choose to collaborate, all rich families do. Why should it be different for the Fus? I heard the Japanese are very cruel people. After all, one doesn't become wealthy by saving, does he."

But then one day, her husband changed his mind.

"Soon every Chinese is going to drink from the same river as the sea urchins. Not me! Not the Fus! I hate the ungrateful imitators. Pit viper playing dragon."

He came up with a plan.

"I once went fishing there. Wuan is a small village on the bend of the Yangtze river, not far from here in case you change your mind. It's a paradise, sheltered in the lush green beyond the hilly horizon; a heaven of scented grass, hidden far, far away from the sulphur of arms. So what do you say, Butterfly? Doesn't the place sound just like the Tang poems you wrote in your calligraphy?" And she answered, mimicking the light-hearted, tuneful voice he had employed for a laugh: "*Lotuses lean on each other, laughing and weeping. Shalalala. Under the eaves the swallow rests, looking over the hills to two yellow birds singing in the one inch of love's shadow.* Let's pack."

She didn't mention that the poem was not by Consort Ban or Li Po but one of her own, neither did she know of its consequence. She had no idea that when she drafted the effortless words, someone was saluting her from a close distance.

It was Fate's hand.

Father, mother and son packed on the same day. They left without telling anyone, except a childless couple, Mr. and Mrs. Chow, who joined them at the waterfront where the boat waited for the two couples and one son to get on and disappear. Her husband said he and Mr. Chow had discovered the paradise Wuan together when trekking along the river, fishing.

"At his age Sheng needs to have his own secrets," so she tried to convince her husband. "I know the Urchins will arrive in Nanking any day now, but surely not on such a lovely day!"

The mild sun of early summer was shining early on the morning. From the hilltop, the river was a perfect parabola shaped by two silvery, hugging arms of water. In fact, Yangtze is a masterpiece of calligraphy, she thought to herself. It is a stroke of genius put there by a masterly hand of light and dark –

Calligraphy was her art. When she held a loaded brush in her hand, she could feel the crushing weight of life, the sadness, the happiness, which she was about to let go in a breath of meditation. Calligraphy was the art of breathing and living, it made her mind clear and lucid. The shining shield with which she defied the dark world and embraced life. For the sake of a metaphor, she would collect fallen petals in the woods and prepare her own ink from them. After she brought home the remains of seasonal plants, she would rub them down her body while bathing. Then she would put on a nightgown and go to bed in wet hair and the pearly, pale leaves clung to her sultry skin. She pitied the seasons that waste away, in her sleep she felt her own life escaping through her pores like essence oil to fuse with the Creation. When she woke up in the morning, she would wipe off the flowery flakes with her undershirt and soak them in soot-black ink. She drew in the fragrant blossoms of this thorny existence. She smelt her skin clothed in the mystery she grew part of, the blue oyster, the lemon dew, the white pigeon's playing toes, the curve of teacup with a lover's lips left on the rim, the dimple of skin on a rainy day...She touches them through her words, pleasantly pungent, like words should be. The dense, shadowy scent of ink comforted her and made her heart beat faster. Calligraphy is her lover, brother and child, all in one. She needed them all. She needed her writing.

So it happened six years ago today, their son Sheng boarded the sampan ferry across the bend, which would glide down-river through the flooded forest and floating villages to Mr. Lau, who had a house at the dockside. She took care that the calligraphy scroll wouldn't be ruined by damp during the Yangtze crossing. It had rained the night before. The river coursed among the hills, washing all the way down to the coast. The violent flow reminded her of muddy tears on a sad, cheerless face. It would take fewer hours than usual to arrive in Nanking.

"See you this evening then, my big son." She had waved to Sheng a goodbye which turned out to be farewell.

In the afternoon, she looked out her window, over the hills, past the brilliant bending water. A flash of premonition made her freeze with disquiet. Rushing to the roof, she searched the horizon, her eyes tracing after a leaf of boat wafting along the river seaward to distinguish, minute and far away, the grey water clouded slowly a deep purple, as if summer berries had been poured in to be wasted. A thought stirred her mind. She almost choked on a formless smell seeping out a rupture of her mental agility.

Sheng did not return in the evening nor the next day or the days after. A few weeks later a man arrived in the village. He was one of the few who survived during the Nanking Massacre.

This is the story he told:

The Chinese troops were no match for their opponents. At dawn the Japanese army took the city by surprise. The military moved quickly and ended up in control of great swathes of the Chinese territory. The slaughter and bloodshed started out on a large scale to suit men's needs. The hunting season has started. This is a hunting game. Nanking is the fair hunting ground for humans in pursuit of quarry.

Hunters take down everything passing in the streets. Shooters barking like a pack of mad dogs, contending to kill the most Chinese, efficiently, getting up to speed, becoming more and more efficient with every teardrop that has fallen. Every teardrop is a dried-up waterfall. Apathetic faces barely know what they do, barely have counted many days of life, fight to the very ending of the day. Hurry up quick, quick. There is more work to finish, this is work like any work is no more than an administrative detail. It is an Imperial order. The Emperor has empowered a hostile policy and approved of every step to victory without hesitation. Every man who kills easily, quickly and in as great numbers as possible shall be honoured. Declothed women and children, down on their knees, stretching out their hand, begging for mercy from Doom – Doom don't fail – begging for a glimmer of hope from an unheard deity singing her old weary song, her old mute requiem: forgive, forgive, we will we might, through the graves of all lands that report around the world the facts and numbers of the dead in a book called History. Out of a torn page

A one-year-old is crawling from under the sewer top, where it was hidden, to suckle on cold nipples of a pair of headless, cold breasts lying on the street, pale and soiled like waste paper, in whose uninterrupted silence

A vast amount of civilians are caught, are taken prisoner to be lined up in front of their dilapidated homes to become targets for bayonet practice for the junior participants of a killing sport. It's the best game they have ever played! Let's turn the music up and shut the world out. Let's hurt them really bad. The party-goers in guns, uniform and fancy pants, once they get tired of wows and everything, set fire to the mutilated bodies tossed into a freshly dug pit. Visions of gore, lamenting, seeking, always, to escape death. Wailing body parts, chased and hunted, burning on a slow fire, scuttling through streets poisoned by gunfire and tattering beats of machine guns buck buck buck rumbling like New Year's firework through

Silent walls of human bodies, charred and maimed beyond recognition. Mute death piling up around every street corner, twisting and shitting on the wordless killing field. No-one heard their eternal screams through the City of Silence, in whose blind disgrace

A woman is holding a baby on her right arm and another on her left. The armed men force her to choose between bad and worse, then stab into her children as if decorating two pumpkins for Halloween. They gang rape the mother and shove her children, still alive and breathing, into a trash bag. Together with her fractured body they are ditched into a shallow grave ready to be closed...And somewhere only we know, somewhere out there we remember

In a secured quarter, a stray gang stops a group of school girls on their way home for afternoon tea. One after another, sadistic men under imperial rule, prattling on telling dirty jokes, cigarette dangling from lips, humiliate them. A ten-year-old girl refuses to take them in her mouth, she is beaten to death with their rifle butts. Her blood can't find quick enough the creases in the shredded, naked flesh of the good Earth to hide. There is a river of blood, a crimson ribbon, hundreds of thousands of ribbons, riddles of life, they have their plans, choking on screams and horror's let-down hair, skirting the islands made of body remains, hurrying aimlessly towards

The dockside facing the ancient harbour in golden sunset. Fishermen's boats and sampans rocking in the ancient water of abandoned sadness like the face of a beloved from yesterday, darkened soon by an ever-increasing shadow. A pyramid built of corpses, all young men with nowhere to hide, nowhere to run, executed in fewer than ten minutes in the final trumpet hour

When the curtains of evening are closing down in order to forget, and the crescent moon is touching the edges of fair *roses covered in very last teardrops, the exhausted, blistered nine-heavens make an effort to end a lurid live show, deafened by exaltation of victors' cheering along the quiet riverbanks. And their "banzai!" cries carry on with a gust of wind and enter the ears of the lanky blind ancient gods idling at twilight and losing their mind. The night blackens the shadows and mute echoes of still vibrant emotions. The Yangtze sunk into an unnatural sleep, shrouded by unsolid mists and clots of body fluids like sanguine roses of oblivion—*

At this point, she stood up. She didn't wait for the story to finish. She walked away without any expression in her face. She was beyond sad, beyond terrified or shocked. She was beyond any of the emotions a human face is capable of expressing. When she came back, she couldn't speak anymore. That day she lost her speech not because she is not allowed to lie in life. She lost it so she would never ever HAVE to tell the stories herself.

For one year long she didn't dare to fall in sleep, fearing she would dream. As soon as she dosed off, she was roused by the stench of burnt hair and flesh, panting, screaming in a voice she didn't have.

In her endless waking hours, she tried to bring back the day that gods looked away from human race, with ink strokes on rice paper. She pictured her son. She looked into his eyes and asked him how he died. She looked through his eyes to see what he saw. She thought what he thought in his last moment. Her strong fingers touched his riddled face buried under a pyramid of dead heads. She wanted to comfort them one by one. She wanted to remember the marred, unrecognised faces and never forget. *Never!* She wanted to capture her son's memory with her writing brush. She ended up with an empty sheet that stayed empty. No trace of black ink on snow white surface, not even a spilled drop. She realised that sorrow was not darkness, neither was it anything like cold icicles as the old saying goes. Grief is madness and emptiness. A bareness that eats into the heart, drinks from the soul, and consumes the last breath of life until nothing is left. No pain: no nothing but naked starkness!

Ever since then her husband had forbidden her to touch rice paper. His own mother sent our son to death! You are a hen who knows nothing of caring for your eggs! She accepted all said about her. She punished herself by enduring whatever punishment he put her through. But her *art* – as he took to task as if chewing on a wasp – she needed it more than ever, not only as a tool to communicate with others now that she couldn't speak. The inky strokes reminded her of the twigs and leaves drifting along the Yangtze. She held onto them without letting go, for otherwise she would lose her only chance to survive. They were two drowning people holding onto two different buoys, torn apart by their pain.

"What is THIS?"

The voice startled her, realigning her with the here and now. She looked up to find her husband holding the calligraphy piece. The soaked paper was still dripping tea, brown rings flourishing like tropical flowers on white. He must have taken it from her breast pocket while her mind was far away with her son. Now he held her handwriting to his eyes. He lifted his face to scrutinise her, mumbling something, and his jaw dropped. The rice paper was covered with a secret writing he didn't know, nor would any sane man! He gazed upon her, silent, his mouth pursed, like a doctor weighing the opinions for his terminal patient. Finally his wife has gone mad! She even devised this impossible writing for the lunatics in her head!

The clock on the wall ticked away. Tick-tack tick-tack. The constant never, creeping in petty pace.

If one could only kill time without injuring eternity, she said without saying. Time stays, *we* go. Love me, my husband.

"Tell you what, Wife," he spoke in a cold voice. "I had luck today. It's *huge*. Cut one piece for the Chows and bring it to them. Fresh air will do you good."

He brushed past her curled up in a ball on the floor, and left.

In the yard she found the slick and leathery creature swimming round the water butt. *Guardian spirit of the Yangtze.* When they arrived in the village, a fisherman's wife told her that the dolphins came every year to the natural shelter in the bending to mate. There is a local legend about dolphin males trying their shotgun with pearl diving girls, said the woman, grinning. The Yangtze Valley is an ancient saucer full of secrets.

Her eyes following the baby dolphin playing in rain water, her hand reached for the cleaver to hold it. It weighed a ton. For a few minutes she didn't move. A raspy female singing voice made her turn her head, the sunny tune seeping out the closed windows of her husband's bedroom upstairs. She saw the formless silhouette behind the dusty glass panes, her husband was watching her to carry out the job, and at his back, the rasping song of the female flowing from the infected gramophone record, luminously unreal, toing and froing, swinging merrily along muffled, suffocating watery chords drifting up on hot waves of air from the river:

Summertime
And the livin' is easy
Fish are jumpin'

...

"One day I'm going to steal the music, all of it," she thought to herself.

She moved her arm. The blade hung over her head. She shut her eyes, her hand plunging through the air, cutting sunbeams, shattering the liquid surface to pieces. Anger seized her. Her eyes jerked wide open in a struggling spasm. Clenching the blade in both her hands, her arms raised again and again like a drum player. They didn't stop until no life was left but grey water clouded slowly a deep purple, as if summer berries had been poured in to be wasted.

The key creaks in the lock. Whispers. She heeds a voice drawing close from ages away. Suddenly it enters her ears:

"Is anyone there? Can you hear me?"

She keeps her eyes shut. Probably another dream, a dream in a dream. How long has it been since last time she heard a human voice, she wonders.

"WHO ARE YOU? How long have you been here?" The voice, gentle, persistent.

"I was dreaming...my other life..." she answers in silence. It was in the summer nearly seventy years ago that she decided she would never speak again. But now she longs to talk to someone. She wants to hold onto her story for the last time.

Leaning over the bed, the man in a long white jacket sees the lips stir, where neither sound nor bubbles emerge. Only creatures from the water could look this old and this fantastic, Reigan thinks. He studies her shade through the golden, orange light encircling her entire body in a magnificent ring. The arms look human, with bared skin cool and velvety to the touch, he speculates. She is wearing a cocktail dress made of a fabulous, wetsuit-tight material, the sexiest dress he has ever seen. It took Reigan a second look to be sure that the sequins are *squama*: scales and tails. Covering all the way up to her neck and shoulders is fish skin, marrow of a fairytale. Director Lai was right, this cannot be an illness. Or if it were it is so fantastic a malady, and so completely absurd it must exist for the sake of imperfection. Perfection through imperfection, this is how the organic system called life works, the pearly tear of the shellfish, the hectic glow of consumption etcetera etcetera.

"Dr. Reigan, I presume?" The voice escapes her throat, surprising her – and him.

Reigan looks into the huge eyes looking back at him.

"What's your name?" he speaks in a tender voice. He can't help feeling drawn to the attractive idea that some fantasy creature is lying stretched in front of him like Goya's odalisque who lost her way in *St. Elsewhere*, waiting for her Dr. Zhivago to heal her body, mind and soul. This is not possible, not in a million years, not even when he mixed science with plenty of beer the night before!

With her long rousing fingers she beckons him to come closer – she has the same hands as Alice. In the left corner of her fish mouth wonderfully shimmering, Reigan notices a beauty mark, not too high and not too low, not too big and not too small. An imperfection exactly right.

"Ca…Cara…Carassiu…s… au…ra…" the mermaid voices, struggling to make herself understood, the mark of desire dancing shy in the corner of her mouth.

"Carassius Auratus Auratus?" Reigan helps her finish the unspoken syllables. *Latin for goldfish.*

Not wasting one more second, Reigan turns to the door and starts to run. Corpses and zombies don't scare him, but this. This absolutely freaks him because of the notion he might be losing it, losing his grip on reality –

He is losing his head.

"I'm upstairs, Dr. Charming – "

Alice's voice is calling from the dark, followed by a splashing sound of water. A tap turns on and off. She is taking a bath.

Reigan walks to the window. He puts out his head to heed the rumbles of life in the street, *like a rumbling sea*, he thinks. He closes the window, draws the curtains and leans over to put on the light. For a few moments he stares into the lime shade until his eyes hurt. Pain can't be unlived. Pain is the bitter potion, the breaking of the shell for him to heal the sick. He believes in pain how terribly morbid it sounds. You gotta love livin', baby! The more said about life's sores the better, *China*! Turning and tossing his jacket onto the couch, he waits for the light-weight fabric to spread soundless on the blue velvet like a creature in a dismal state of mind. He ascends the stairs.

"Mind the warning sign, Doctor Heart attack," Alice yells again from the bathroom, cracking up in giggles. "Blinding beauty, light dimmed for your safety. Today my left breast is slightly smaller but is still very fond of you. Please smile to both of them."

In the semi-dark Reigan spots the milky sheen of her moist body encircled by a steaming aura sphere. *A warning sign*. She is. Perhaps all women in the world are like a hidden island waiting for Vasco Da Gama to discover her dangerous, humbling beauty. His hand finds the light switch next to the door.

"You look definitely better with the light off, Doc. Did something happen at the hospital?" Throwing a quick glance at him, his wife enquires, large eyes still laughing defiantly.

"This heat wave, damn it. Where is the bloody rain? Or typhoon. I love the typhoon." Pause. "I've been *called* to the morgue today."

"You mean you were attacked by a flesh-hungry zombie?"

"How did you know? I hope I won't infect you. Bad disease. It was *brilliant!*" Reigan watches the bathing Ophelia burst into a sparkly peal of laughter, her radiant face dripping water. This woman is amazing. Leaning against the cool tile wall, he follows her every move while mulling over what he just said.

Called, he said. Come to think of it, what happened today feels that way. Why *him*? How did the director decide that this time it's not a skin disease, like the treeman. Instead his boss was determined that mermaid is an extreme case of nervous disorder which has never been explored before let alone seriously studied in any known academic records. The director trusted Reigan to carry out the research work. He counted on detailed report on a regular basis.

"Do you know what clinical lycanthropy means?" Reigan asks dryly, feigning a casual voice.

His wife doesn't answer, beckoning him with her long rousing fingers.

"Any plan to do check-up on me today, Doctor? I'm burning with the worst chemical romance, highly contagious mystery virus – "

"…Syndrome of werewolf involves a delusion that he or she has transformed into an animal or that he or she *is* an animal, either a wolf or…"

"Come to bath, I will make you forget *her* – It's her, isn't it?"

Amazing, this female intuition.

"It's past midnight, sweet lady. I just want to talk a little, that's all. Good night!" Yawning significantly, he walks over bending down to kiss her damp hair.

"I'm very ill. *Please save me,* Doctor – "

Half risen from her place, she squeezes her soaked, slippery body to his, leaning her entire weight against him, pulling him to her to connect their lips together. Reigan feels her heat through his thin summer clothes. Eyes closed with his both arms strained behind her dark, glossy, long hair, he slumps falling over the edge with huge splashing water.

"Shhh – "

Reigan feels her sharp little teeth, her tongue twisting around his. His body thawing out, a burst of adrenaline rises in his throat, all his senses are tuned in, clear and magnified in balmy liquid tickling at his flared skin. They are drowning, falling slowly into the abyss of savouring delight. Gulping for air, his heart drumming on a shallow surface, he hauls her up by her hair. She guffaws with trembles, breathing heavily, her swift hands moving to unbutton him. Her long rousing fingers are closed on his stirred sex to become the shape of a weird flower.

"I don't mind you are in love with a werewolf, Doctor," she wheezes in his ear. "Let's need each other. Let's make babies. Lots of babies, like fishes do. *What?* What's wrong?"

She takes his hand back to touch her flushed, heaving breasts.

"I think we talked about this before." Drawing away, Reigan pushes himself up. "We can't have children. Not now, Alice."

"Why not? I'm horny, you too as far as I can see."

"You and me, our careers. Think, Alice."

"As a matter of fact I did some thinking tonight. Damn my career, and yours too," she says quietly. "I want some real shit to happen in our life."

"What's the *real shit*?"

"A family. Kids. I don't want to wind up like Mademoiselle Coco." A large teardrop oozes from the corner of her eyes, threading down her pretty, wet face.

Reigan feels tremendously sorry. He had wanted to say it's not the career. To have children you need to trust the world, and he is not sure about that. He turns his head, pretending to study a bottle of something on the edge.

"What is THIS?"

Frozen in place, he tries to focus his water stinging eyes on a strange pattern on her skin, orange and pearly flakes.

"Our make-up artist did it. He was trying out body paint for our new show. We call it Goldfish series, waterproof. What do you think? Oh baby you are cold – "

The shiny, scaled arm extends to turn on the hot water.

"I'm okay, just a little tired. Tomorrow is another crazy day," Reigan mutters, his teeth chattering. Stepping on unsteady legs, he heads out of the door, leaving a series of wet steps on the dark stone floor. He forgot to dry.

The clock on the bedside table reads 2:55 AM. Reigan hasn't slept a wink. Next to him Alice snores softly, her arm curled on her side, fish scales glitzy and powdery in the pallid light from the street lamps. He stares in her face for a while. Putting out a finger to remove gently the leftovers of dark mascara on her lashes, he furrows. His mind flashes back to the morgue. That was ludicrous! He had wanted to hug the dead woman and pump life into her cold body. How typical, maniac doctor having a thing for a juicy corpse, and he keeps telling himself he has not gone mad. Shalalala TUM! Great!

He slips out of bed. He is dying for a cigarette.

Downstairs he finds his jacket lying limp and vulnerable on the couch. Rummaging through pockets, he remembers he quit seven days ago. His finger touches something. He reaches over to turn on a reading light.

In his palm lies a sheet of fan-shaped paper. He has never seen anything like it before. How did it get in there in the first place? The rice paper is tinted an aged brown. Not the factory-made thingamajig they produce in tons of rolls a day but handmade piece by piece any calligraphy artist would pawn his heart for. He knew it because his father once showed him a fan-shaped sheet just like this one he had stored for years. "King of paper, made from silk tree leaves. Manuscripts written on these sheets last for thousands of years, no crack no rupture no nothing," his father had said. He wanted his son to draw on it and make houses ever everlasting as the piece of paper.

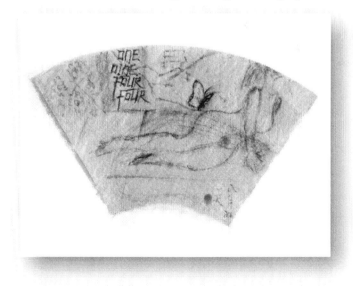

... a secret writing meant only for the eye of its maker

Reigan examines the fan in his hand with his keen eye for detail and a heartbeat in every line and dot, as if he *feels* her breath coming off the yellowed surface. The simple strokes give a picture of a woman, her face half hidden due to composition, her nude body swaddled in a wispy trace of fabric. Who is she posing for? Who is she looking at through her omitted eyes? She has an impious air about her that he finds exhilarating. She is reclining on some sort of framework, which – Reigan suddenly realises with a start – is the tatami flooring. Behind her, the silhouette of a butterfly alights on a twig that has grown into the window framing the distant hills. All done in soot-black ink. Nice job. This is the easy part. *But what does the writing mean?* At first sight it looks like a fancy squiggle, some sort Korean or Japanese. The ink marks are definitely not Chinese. The handwriting is heavily stylised. It is a riddle, a secret writing meant only for the eye of its maker.

He walks up to the bookshelf, and pulls out 1001 Handwritings, an encyclopaedia of calligraphy brainteasers through the dynasties. He carries the five kilogram volume back to the couch where he parks himself.

Quaquaversal!

Reigan awakes to the sudden sound and opens his eyes, which he closes immediately in the intense morning sun pouring through a crack in the curtains. The handwriting book has dropped to the floor, pages spread out face-down. Apparently he fell asleep while studying dynastic obscurities in writing styles. He searches for the fanned paper. His brows knitted, his eyes linger on the grainy, antique coloured surface for some seconds. Something dawns on him. *He knows.*

He gathers the book from the floor and paces into the kitchen to make some coffee. Alice has left for work. The note on the counter says she will be late this evening. She didn't wake him because he looked so cute. And there is steamed bread and noodle soup in the fridge.

Reigan pours some hot water in a cup with instant coffee. He removes the Post-It from the wall and reads the line he jotted down yesterday. "How inappropriate to call this planet earth when it is quite clearly Ocean." A woman's heart is a deep ocean of secrets. *Chezchez la femme, pardieu!* Look for the woman. Teach me the guilty details.

He finishes the black liquid in one. No sugar, he likes the bitter taste in the heart. He rushes upstairs for a quick shower. Brushing his teeth, he looks in the mirror, turning left and right to make sure he still has his head. You never know.

He dresses himself, locks the door, gets in to the car and speeds off.

He almost bumps into someone as he hurries out of the lift.

"Good morning, Dr. Reigan! Missed your flight this morning?" Nurse Lyn smiles at him brilliantly, eyes shining with mischief.

"Sorry Lyn, I'm late. Listen. Can you check if Director Lai is in today? Tell him I need half an hour. Your lift, where are you going, up or down?"

The nurse doesn't move, eyeballing him with a funny look on her face. Reigan tucks on his tie, checks buttons, rubs in his stubbly face. Somewhere a clock is ticking, the pace of the inevitable.

"Director Lai died one month ago," she says in a low, slow voice. "We went to his funeral together. You are our supervisor until we find a new director, Dr. Reigan."

"Yeah…of course. I mean…*How?*"

"How did he die? Migraine and vomiting. Then, fever killed the old man. He passed away in peace though."

"Oh right…The heat huh?…We often listened to music together. Jazz. He was very kind, treated me like a son. I think I caught a cold…" Reigan pronounces a stretch of disjointed words, tugging at his collar to allow himself to breathe.

"…Lyn? Do you know where I can find a television? Not flat screen. I need an old-fashioned stand-alone, with glass funnel in the front like a time tunnel." Reigan makes a distracted gesture, drawing a picture in the air of what could have been anything.

"You mean one that looks like a fish tank when switched on?"

"Precisely. How do you know?"

"I think I saw one in the broom cupboard. I'll check if it works."

"You do that. It goes to your recommendation."

"Thanks. I will bring it to your office. See you in a bit, Dr. Reigan."

The nurse turns to call the lift.

Entering his office, Reigan dashes to his desk in a few great leaps. Reaching out to switch on the computer with mechanical, mindless routine, he drops down in the swivel chair, his back soaked in a cold, cold sweat. For a few moments he sits stock still, lifeless and unmoving, staring blankly into the bright screen in front of his face. Gregor Samsa skulks into his mind. Kafka's creation knew his old self was gone after he woke up one morning to find that his human body was transformed into a monstrous cockroach. He, on the other hand, doesn't have a clue where this all leads. Gregor accepted the circumstances, soon he would find out how people really are. Reigan hopes that by accepting his condition – whatever it may be – this lunacy will take him to a major discovery. Odd, he doesn't feel mad at all. And as far as he can know, his head plus familiar features still sits on his good old shoulders. He checked that in the mirror this morning.

"Come in!"

Nurse Lyn appears with her back turned, pushing the door wide open, hugging in her arms something big and clumsy.

"I got your fish tank. Give me a hand."

They place the imitation wood TV set in the window sill.

"You need these too." The nurse extracts some dull grey cables from a plastic bag she has with her covered in dusty cobweb.

"You are my sunshine, Lyn. Did you watch?"

"Black and white. Looks a bit film noir but it will work. Enjoy yourself, *Dr. Caligari*."

She closes the door behind her, then opens it. "O, don't forget the bunny aerials," she says, and disappears.

"Is anyone there? Can you hear me?" Reigan whispers.

The feverish aura around her body has significantly reduced in size as well as intensity. For the first time he can see her clearly through the cool orange shade. Lying there in the bed is not Little Red's grandma, she looks deceptively young. But what an absurd idea! Fish simply don't get old by adding folds in the skin. An enigmatic expression dons her inscrutable face without a crinkle, her wide eyes puzzled by their own ageless ambiguity like Italian marble. Reigan just *knows* she is very, very old, perhaps too old to be still alive. This is what he found out about the creature lying in the hospital bed in front of him. His first breakthrough last night when he was trying to solve the riddle of the fanned paper. But there is more to it than he could possibly imagine.

Something has changed about her since he fled the room last time, almost screaming. Her body, fluent as one ink stroke, is small and sweet shaped, lending a yearning, heartbroken sweet-sourness to her fantail, ribbed, spilled, overflowing ink satin clouds. Reigan recalls the taste of sweet and sour flavoured crisps he had last night to keep himself awake, with a blaze of hot chilli that tasted like gravity's rainbow. She seems excited, rid of the tedium of silence, allowing herself to come out of the shadow of the unspeakable, a memory in the making. She is in the restless, reckless mood of a devious young girl waiting to cut the Gordian knot of TRUTH.

"But…terf…ly," she mutters, difficultly reviving the muscles of her rigid tongue that have lost their spring.

"Butterfly! Nice to meet you! Guess what, Butterfly? I know your secret you are hiding. I solved your riddle."

Reigan digs his hand in the side-pocket of his workwear.

"When I was here last time, you slipped this to me so I would be your partner in crime. Well, you got me under your spell. This is never easy, but if you want to tell me when you are ready, I'm all ears."

"Am…Amne…sia…" her gorgeous mouth stirs, voicing shredded sounds. Her long rousing finger touches to the brown surface of rice paper held to her face. The fidgety fingers are joined by an opaque, quavering web. Heedfully, they trace along the flailed fringe of the fanned paper, and stop at the secret writing in soot-black ink.

Reigan smiles, raising a triumphant voice:

"The glyph on this six thousand year old piece of art says: one nine four four. It's English. See? I figured out. Simple plain English but written in such a manner that the four tiny ink clusters *appear* like Chinese pictograms! Secret language is love's secret domain. The night's invisible garden where sick roses blossom that can't bear to see the daylight! You want me to help you remember a dark secret you are so ashamed of that you needed to forget. Or perhaps it is something we all have forgotten because the memory of it would mean so much pain. Amnesia is the "missing link" of memory, repressed memory caused by traumatic experiences. These days there are a great many books about trauma and its effects on our country's one point three billion poor souls. Poppycock recipe. We are the aristocrats privileged with a past. I suggest we pick up where we left off. Let's find your

Wu Shan Man. So tell me, Butterfly, what is it *exactly* you don't want to remember?"

As soon as he hears the inexpert, diagnostic flow of words pouring through his mouth, Reigan is shocked. One single remark, one mistake like this would cause more nervous blocks and raise further objections to finally break last tendons of the easily broken, delicate mind.

The bed creaks. The sheet curves and bulges, revealing more of her scaled body shape, joggling oddly. Instead of resistance which Reigan should have expected, he hears the laborious tongue speak again.

"When I was thirty...nine, something hap...happened...I couldn't s...speak... for...got – "

The measured, stiff voice gulps for air as if she would soon be submerged by the many words spoken at once. A ripple of pain disturbs the calm shining, a large teardrop trickling down her hyaline face.

"One...nine...four...four...is...a... y...year – "

1944, the year when stardust fell and she stopped dying.

Summer, 1944

On the early summer day nearly seventy years ago, she obeyed her husband and did what he had asked her to do. In her nature she had kept something wild and untamed, something very precious in a young girl which she is bound to lose when she grows older. As she raised the cleaver in her hands and cut the fish playing round the water cask, she would never forget the haunting blue of the sky, so remote and so incredibly unreal like the moon from the Tang Dynasty. But yet it was real, tombstone real and weighing heavy on her heart. And in the background, a raspy female voice singing the forever joyful song, *summertime*.

The village Wuan was separated in two equal parts by the Yangtze's water running through her heart: *hush~~hush~~hush~~*

The Chows lived on the other side of the hills. Once they arrived, the two couples took the two houses available, the Chows on the upper bank, the Fus and their son on the lower bank. They didn't know when the war was going to end and had agreed to share their food in times of shortage.

She wrapped the chunk of fish meat in oil paper.

She had walked the entire route through the woods many times before and explored its maze-like twists and turns. Last time she took a shortcut to the chasm. She went onto the bridge made of timber slats on frayed ropes. When she looked down to the uncharted landscape, her heart stopped. She saw herself fly above the earth towards the air with no one trying to tie her down. From the unsteady height, suddenly, she spotted the silhouette of a house under the shadow of cultivated growths. The plants were once trimmed in splendid clusters but now they were left to the will of nature. She had passed the hidden grounds before, drawn by the curious waves from somewhere inside. A hand through cornstalks, she imagined. Or it was a chorus made up of rustling taffeta skirts on dance floor surrounded by gilded mirrors? Her breath hitched in her throat. She couldn't quite explain it, even though one part of her was unwilling to know for sure. She wondered whether it was the sea she heard, or the expectation of the sea. *Shalalala*.

Carrying the food parcel in her hand, she entered the woodland. It was a windless day, no leaf stirred and no sounds except for the twittering chitchat of birds that brought cool to the sultry hour. She decided to walk to the "sea" in the pink-roofed house she saw the other day from the bridge.

She found the path upholstered by giant grass and followed the direction for a while. The pathway forked. Indecisive which to choose, she halted her pace to listen to a peculiar birdsong. It's a mockingbird. But how is this possible? These perching birds are found only in the New World. As a child she often visited a bird collector with her aunt. She would spend hours in his house alone and listen to the sounds of the rare bird the man proudly owned in his mixed bag of a collection. Many years later she would realise that her aunt had an adulterous relationship with the bird man, and the child played red herring.

The songbird started again, after it suspended for a few impatient minutes. She detoured from her course to find out. When she came to a clearing at last, the sight in front of her took her breath away.

A lotus pond stretching up against an emerald slope, on whose gentle rise the bright pink of roof flourished, a gigantic blossom among ruthless green, extravagantly wild, isolated by its geography to be able to prosper. A summer breeze blew over the scented hillside from a distance that pleases the eye, bringing the umbrellas of silent leaves to a soothing thrill of murmurs. She found her sea! *Shalalala*.

She left the fish on the cobbled narrow edge of the pond and approached the house. She didn't think she had a choice.

The house was abandoned by its former owner, for reasons she could well fathom. Colonial style, white plaster balustrade, veranda in the shades. In the outskirts of the city, there were many vacant houses like this one, lonesome landmarks which reminded her of a line from a Fado:

"*É meu e vosso este fado destino que nos amarra…*"

The door was unlocked. She followed the hallway to the end. She entered a large room, baffled, puzzled. The impressive space seemed to expand forever by the grace of French windows flanking on both sides of the shadowed walls. Muted sunlight filtering through green shutters. Crystal tears dangling from a big chandelier tree, playing weightless gazing eyes on the floor dressed in stone-grey tatami. The room breathed a gentle fragrance of oblivion. She speculated what kind of person had once lived here, before the war drove him away. A German scholar who had travelled to Japan to find treasures which he brought back to his safe haven? An American businessman who married a Japanese woman he had met at a nightclub on the Bund?

Her attention was attracted by the closet buried in the shadows.

The sliding door was half closed, showing the chock-full inside. The wardrobe smelt of damp. She pushed a little open, her fingers leafing through an array of garments. Tailored suits, shirts, a woman's evening dress on a hanger with an address (Nanking Road 68, Shanghai), complete with gloves and satin tights. Her hand doved to touch the golden kimono hung up next. She scrutinised the subtle embroideries in the lining, hundreds of flowery petals flit, fly, float, sunset snow. With one twirl of her finger the costly silk fell cool and heavy in her palm. She was dazed by its secretive shine, her heart tantalised, pounding in her mouth. Before she could think she had paced to the midst of the vast, clear space, the piece of shimmering gold trailing behind her.

She undressed herself, peeling the thin summer dress off her body. The dress hugged her form, too tight, and the fabric had turned stiff after many washings. It feels as if she took off a chimney she had been wearing for ages. Holding her breath, she pulled her white cotton shorts down past her knees, letting it drop to the floor around her ankles. She did all this with slow, minimal movement, quietly, without making any sound. Standing in the murky light, naked, her eyes shone with a speckled brilliance to match two small white rice seed pearls in her ears. She felt her skin burn, and slipped into the cool, lavish silk.

The robe was tailored for a man's body or a big woman, she could barely walk without stumbling on the golden ripples circled at her feet. She decided to lie down, right on the spot, which she did, quietly, without making any sound. Closing her eyes, she listened to the sea of leaves outside. She felt the fabric under her, frail and light as cloud. She felt the knitted patterns of the tatami flooring pressing through in her soft flesh. It was a long time since she felt her body, tranquil weight, every pain seemed to ebb away and fade.

As if to be sure she was still there, she slipped her hand through the slit on the front to touch herself. Her belly, moving up and down as she breathed. Her hand strayed, lower, passing an austere lean ridge. She froze, fever ruffled her heart. Her breath quickening, her hand started to move again, travelling into the deeper darkness. She moaned, her body roamed over the scented straw flooring, squirmed, her eyes charged with life. Wave of desire deluged her, intoxicating wine. The cries welled in her throat that she held back –

She felt exhausted. The desire to live exhausted her, the desire light as a butterfly but strong as a pine. She fell asleep instantly, listening to the sea of leaves outside the walls. *Shalalala.*

A sound awoke her. She looked around, disoriented at first. Then, she recognised the interior. She rose slowly. Tucking the silk carefully around her body, making sure she wouldn't trip over, she followed the hallway to the kitchen. She searched in the drawers and found what she looked for. Following the way back, she crossed the vast, clear space to the shadows at the far end of the room. In her hand she held a knife. She had found two knives in the kitchen drawers, one for meat which was too heavy. The one she chose had an elegant straight line like a rapier. Probably for cutting the watermelons, she deduced.

With one sweeping arm she threw open the wardrobe. She waved the metal blinking sharp and cold in her hand. The stooped figure moved behind the wall of clothes. Stepping out the half-light, a young man stood up in front of her. He was pale and all in a tremble like a leaf on a cold wintry tree. She didn't know that out there in the world there was still someone more helpless than she –

"Who is he?" Reigan butts in, interrupting her story.

Whatever *she* is, this creature certainly knows how to weave a story, vivid with details. He wants to know if she blushes sometimes. But a goldfish does the blushing thing all the time. What mystifies Reigan the most is that, as soon as she started to tell her story, she forgot to stutter. Her sense of urgency has overthrown her dread. Despite the fine weaving garnished with pearly jewels and sprigs hot and spicy – as if to make her memory more sufferable, to kill the pain with the tingle of sedation in the spine – the shadow of terror lurks in every corner of her tale. Reigan sensed that from the very beginning. Demons are as complex and knotty as shoestrings. It's never meant to be Cinderella romantic comedy. *What is she afraid of?*

The pager on his waist makes a beeping noise. Reigan takes a look at his watch and realises that he missed the meeting with a young researcher and two psychiatrists. Now a journalist from the state news agency is waiting for him in his office. These guys do keep unreadable stories coming.

"Sorry, I have to run. I brought you this to keep you company."

In a smooth flow of arms Reigan shoves the wheeled table to her bedside, arrays the wires, pulls out the bunny ears and turns the tube to face her.

"Push the red button, the rest is easy. And, in case you are hungry, which I think you are – " he reaches for the shopping bag on the floor, digging out two paperboard packages. "I take it you like popped rice? Let's have a look. Beef or salmon flavour?"

"No…can…nibal…"

"It's all right. I'm not cannibal either."

Reigan opens beef to put in her webbed hand.

She smiles. The best thing she can do with those Angelina Jolie lips, Reigan thinks as he hurries towards the door. He hesitates for a second, then puts the padlock back on the steel shackle.

Reigan sits on the chair he brought along with him. So this is going to be tough. It was less than 24 hours ago that he ran out of the dark, little sickroom, he thought he would never come back again. Yet here he is. He discovered a secret, then anther. Now he is an addict addicted to this marvellous lunacy. Why not? Sick roses are red, real fish leap and dive. Abstract principles won't change, simple as that.

He reaches out to pull on the sheet to cover her bared body. She kicks, punches, wriggles and will sometimes give a brisk knee to the orchid thief in her dreams without warning. Narrowing his eyes, mystified, Reigan studies her shiny torso swinging from shadow to light from light to shadow. With every passing minute she assumes more and more the shape of a real woman, and her face is her own masterpiece of fiction. He waits for her to rouse from a world full of anthropophagous monsters lurking in the abyss of her mind.

Which she did.

"Do they bite? Memory bites and looks like a BIG horse with four teeth left, *chop chop chop*," Reigan remarks brightly, looking deeply into the hazy eyes suddenly split open.

"Ah good, because silence never won rights. *Quid pro quo*. 'Silence of the lambs' is our understanding of human rights in this country we live. Let us rejoice truth. What I want to know. Is *he* coming here?"

She shakes her scales, bamboozled.

"You are waiting for *him*, aren't you? Your aunt, I'm having the cold feet blahs! I know this was the way it would be. Collector of tears make us boogie with gratefulness. Did they drown her alive in the river together with her lover, the bird guy?"

Her eyes widening, she observes him tensely, in disbelief, aghast.

"Do you read dreams, Doctor?"

"Sort of."

"Sort of what?"

"*Somniloquy*. My aha jeweller. I have been sitting here for some hours. You talk, you scream, you giggle, you swear. You seem to have tons of treasure to hide in your sleep. Who is Sheng? You kept shouting his name. You want to talk about him?"

Her eyes expanded from anguish and fear, she looks past him and again meets his eyes.

"Sheng is my son," she mutters in a cracked, barely audible voice.

"Hang on. Are you saying that you had a sexual relationship with your son?! Oh don't tell me you are a stupid fish! When I was a kid I watched a television programme showing all kinds of animal behaviour. There was this aquarium where there lived a big happy fish family. A baby fish grew himself into an adult male, and suddenly one day he decided to chase after his mom and sisters. He practically raped one of them. The results. Well, after several bouts of interbreeding, even the millionfish end up with abnormalities such as bent spines and early death. It was *gross*."

"Do you want to hear or not, Doctor?"

"Indulge me."

Summer, 1944

She waved the knife to the stooped figure in the wardrobe. Stepping out the half-light, a young man stood up in front of her. He was pale and all in a tremble like a leaf on a cold wintry tree. She didn't know that out there in the world there was still someone more helpless than she –

"Poor thing," she thought. She pitied him. She thought of the woman who waited somewhere far away for her son to return, who never returned –

But then, in the young man's eyes she caught a glance that upset her. It was not until months later did she recall their first encounter, she would then realise that she didn't find the pink-roofed house by sheer luck. Unlike our life, accident is a wonderful film actor who never lacks concentration and imagination. The stranger had been preparing for their rendezvous for a long time. He learned everything about her by hiding himself behind bushes. He observed her patiently to know her every fad and folly. And when he was alone at night, he fantasised about the woman whom he stalked day in, day out without losing her sight for a second. Then one day, he went out to the woods and imitated the bird he saw in a movie. It happened because it *had* to happen.

Something in his eyes upset her and troubled her. It was guilt. She knew the anger directed to oneself. Guilt. Not because he saw her naked, but a remorse soaked to the bone, a stain that poisons the heart. She couldn't help but put out her hand to touch the stranger's face that wore the pain unbecoming of its age. Suddenly, she leaned forward to kiss the young man. His eye, her lips tracing the bridge of his lean, straight nose. He stopped breathing, her mouth had found the curve of his mouth. Hesitantly, uncertainly, their tongues met, and locked –

She disentangled herself brusquely, pulling away to look at the stranger from a short distance. She was surprised by herself, by him. Several minutes passed while they stood there, not knowing what to do and where to look. She felt his hand unlocking her fingers. The metal dropped with a crispy sound, gliding brilliantly over the hopscotch flooring. She must have felt happy then, the sound of the knife reminded her of her childhood game! How happiness produces pure nonsense!

He took her hand and led her to the low table near the window, where he sat her down. He pushed the rice paper to her front. *He knew she was mute.* In hindsight this should have alarmed her, but that was not the way it came about.

He loaded the brush in the inkstone and started to write: "My name is…" She stopped his writing hand. Taking the brush from him, she wrote quickly in her elegant handwriting:

I call you Sheng. It means life.

Sheng should be your age if he had lived today, she thought to herself.

"Sheng that is not Sheng," Reigan speaks in a soft voice. "If I recall correctly, your son was eighteen when he died six years before. So the young man should be…"

"Twenty four. I was told so later. He was twenty four years."

"And you were?"

"I told you, I was thirty-nine when my son died."

"So you were forty-five when you two met in that house."

"I know, I could be his mother. Tell you a secret, Doctor," she lowers her voice to a whisper, "my *sort*, we don't age because we don't give up who we are."

"That's not my point."

"Then what's your point?"

"If you were a forty-five-year-old woman in 1944, one year before the war ended, that makes you probably the oldest living person on the face of the Earth. Your sort don't age, but you don't die either."

"May I tell you a story, Doctor?"

"I have no doubt you can! Stick to possibilities, make sure to take risks.'

"I stole this one. Is that enough risk for you?"

"Stolen from whom?'

"The fish tank you brought me."

She raises one arousing finger to point at the glass tube TV. For an instant the image of Alice's hand flashes back to him, her fingers flowering into a swanky orchid on his sex.

Reigan clears his throat. "The fish tank? What about it?"

"Have you noticed I lost my stutter, Doctor? This is how. After you left, I couldn't sleep. So I turned on the aquarium which happened to be a vast ocean – "

"National Geographic Channel. It's my favourite too when I suffer from insomnia. You adopt your pace to the nature, whose wisdom is patience. It works more effectively than sleeping pills. Sleep is the art of patience."

"So I was watching the ocean, a jigsaw puzzle of living beings. Then suddenly, I heard a voice. I heard a story told by a sea tortoise on an extraordinary voyage to lay her eggs across the ocean water."

"What do you mean, *told*?"

"Yes, the ocean has her own language. And yes, I understand it. But humans don't? No. Humans don't understand a thing, do they?"

She smiles her sybaritic smile.

"The sea tortoise told the story to herself, for that's the way to keep her mind focused on her goal which is 11,000 kilometres away, a distance she will cover in 99 days. A world record. Most of all, she has to find food every day and it's not going to be easy. Very often she has to feed herself on stories to appease her hunger, and she needs surprises. She is a true traveller, a true storyteller at heart. She remembers the oldest, strangest tales told of the deep, with wild freedom abhorred by people."

"Why abhorred?"

"You know the reason, Doctor. Fear is a habit of people, freedom is an addiction of the mind. The two needs that contradict, which is why most of us wind up living a tedious life because no-one wants to be called a user. Well then, here it comes, the allegory I previously eavesdropped."

"In the womb of the sea, there is a lake of changing colour. It's a place revered by all sea creatures, one of the last ancient spots harbouring the ancient monsters, dragons, dogfish godzilla, shrieking hordes of medusa, and who knows what. Here the ghastly beings bathe in the tender waves, only sometimes people on the shore spotted them, the tip of a tail, an appalling claw, or some intriguing shades on the colourless surface of water. However, people who guessed that something is going on don't have a clue that underneath the lake, where the monsters loiter and spy on their lives, there stood once a city. This is where T. T. O. has lived for millions of years."

"Tea tea old?"

"No, it's T.T.O. That Thing of the Ocean. God of the immortal, the genie who lives in the abysmal darkness. In the dead of night, shreds of a voice drifted from the layer of volcanic ashes in the deep, deep sea. Words, gurgles, and sniggers, as if somebody is laughing a wicked laugh or drowning. Then a painter arrived on the shore one day. He stayed at an inn. Every morning after breakfast people would find him walking to the sea for a dip. He would stay in water for long hours. After a while, people started to believe that the painter came to look for the monsters to paint them.

"It was late in the afternoon. The sun was setting as usual, the sea was tranquil as usual. But all of a sudden, the weather changed just like that. The sea became so dark, as dark as a blind man's night. On the shore everything seemed calm and peaceful, however. There was no wind at all, the sort preoccupied seascape shortly before the typhoon. The painter felt the overpowering tension in him, not that he was afraid of storms. He *loved* the unhelpful passion, wild, wasted. He was twitchy because the innkeeper told him in the morning that the sea took several lives in the past few days, all excellent swimmers like him. Presently, he thought he had heard something screaming, something trapped in the bowels of darkness. Maybe it's an imprisoned idea, not lost but not free either, the painter considered while climbing up the shore. Uncertain whether to leave or stay, he tarried. At this moment he saw in the corner of his eye a shapeless figure surfacing. It was neither big nor small. It was as it was, *shapeless*. And it carried something across its shoulders, or it was carrying itself, wounded, the weightless weight? He turned to look it in the eye when the shapeless figure dashed towards his direction, shooting through the air like a wet arrow. He shut his eyes and waited. Nothing happened. After a while, he opened his eyes just in time to catch a glimpse of a shapeless shadow disappearing to the end of the day, leaving an elegant trail of footprints in the sand."

"Did he find out what it was?"

"No."

"Listen, Cho Cho san, I have to check my other patients. Tomorrow same time?" Hopelessly addicted; addiction is something Reigan should know about.

"Did he have dark eyes, Sheng who was not Sheng?" he improvises as he prepares to leave.

"Be patient, Doctor. You talked about patience."

"Well, did he?"

"Dark brown eyes, shining straight hair so black it looked blue. He didn't look like a soldier."

"A soldier? I don't remember you mentioned he was a soldier."

"Leave me, Doctor Reigan. Timing is everything. I must rest. This weather makes me drowsy. I can hardly wait for the storm to come."

Reigan walks out the lift to find the corridor empty and dimly lit. Everything looks abandoned, dirty floors, stained walls and a heady, old smell. Everything seems to come straight from the pictures he found yesterday in the archive. Those were great shots of a psychiatric clinic during the Cultural Revolution, the photogenic setting had the haunting beauty of a nightmare. *What the hell is going on?* Every sickroom is supposed to be packed like sardines. How come he never sees a soul, neither doctors nor patients? The offices of his colleagues are permanently closed to their newly installed supervisor. Everybody is hiding from him. Nurse Lyn reported yesterday though that the symptoms abated on a number of patients. The nine-year-old girl with acute photophobia was cured of her morbid fear of light. She asked Lyn to turn on her fairy nightlight when she went to bed, for the first time in weeks.

"Lyn?" Reigan looks into the door around the corner, the first and only door that is open in the entire hospital building. Reigan suppresses his urge to ask questions. Instead he says:

"The conference. Have you cancelled yet? They keep sending me email newsletter."

"Dr. Reigan, are you sure? It's a very important occasion."

"Conferences are for people who are importantly not getting anywhere. Afterwards it's the annual sightseeing in three ancient cities, Peking, Cooking and F…"

Suddenly, Reigan stops to talk. Walking across the room to the window, he stoops to peer through the fishbowl in the windowsill.

"I bought it last week. Pretty, isn't she? I thought it looked like Angelina Jolie. I swear I would be a better person if my girlfriend had one of those lips!" The nurse prattles away cheerfully, curling her mouth to a hilarious shape.

"Your girlfriend, is she an albino too?" Reigan observes, gazing at the creature behind the thin glass wall. He is astounded by the huge fantail wafting and twirling around, white as pigeon.

"The lady at the pet shop said this one had lost her lover to a bacteria, maybe she was pulling my leg. When I was a kid, my mom gave me a goldfish for my birthday. It belonged to a small race and looked like a vermillion comma in the old glass jar where I put it. One morning I woke up to find it dead on the floor. The fish had jumped through the chipped rim of the glass jar and committed suicide! I thought the goldfish must have felt really bad, even as a child I understood that. Why live if you can't? But you know what, Dr. Reigan. Goldfish are like swans, they mate for life. They lose their colour when they feel sad, this is the only thing I remember from biology class. Look, I'm not in the lobby group to put people in jail for speaking their mind, even though that's what makes our country famous in the world. Fortunately, fish don't have a voice, we won't tread on somebody's long toes and get ourselves in trouble. I brought it here, I thought at least it has me. You don't mind, do you, Dr. Reigan?"

"I wouldn't mind turning into a vermillion goldfish myself. Have a good day, Lyn! And don't forget to cancel."

Making his way to the office, Reigan stops at the coffee machine for his caffeine fix he needs to fully function. He sits down at his desk and starts to look through the pile of work he has neglected for the past weeks. He signs a few documents, his mind drifting to the shapeless monster on the beach. *What is T.T.O.*, That Thing Of the Ocean that carries its own disfigured self across its own shoulders?

"If the ocean be the metaphor of the mind," he thinks out loud, "the shapeless shadow is our conscience." Yes, of course! Conscience is the only thing in the world that could be carried by nothing but itself. Conscience keeps more people awake than coffee. It's a confession! Her entire story is an exposé. The patient is scared to remember what happened to her over half a century ago, but only her memory could give her absolution. She has come here to DIE!

Timing is everything, she said. She is waiting for the perfect moment!

She is waiting for *him*.

Summer, 1944

In the beginning she would visit the house only once a week to bring Sheng that was not Sheng some food. Fruit, pickles, and beans that were meant for the Chows. She knew the risk she took but she couldn't watch him starve. She treated him like a mother would her child. She tried. But when alone, she found herself touch him with her mind, drawing the silhouette in the oppressive damp of wardrobe, his face so young yet heartbreakingly aged. She dreamed they were kissing each other like in movies, hidden behind a golden hat he tossed in the air. He gave her small bites on her earlobe and split her pearls, she could see blood on his teeth. When she woke up, she caught herself meditating the shape of his tongue. He tasted like a salted flower, with a sunny shade of saffron with which she would flavour her meals at the dinner table. Frightened by herself, she remembered the first bouquet Sheng had brought home for his mother after playing at the river with his little friends. She thought of the time when she had held her baby boy in her arms, patting him to sleep, absorbing the range of smell rising from the downy mass of hair. An incense of burnt earth mingled with sweat and body heat. Whoever says babies smell fresh as apple is lying. The perfume that breeds the strongest ties, all the rest may be only thwarted passion, sparks from life's electricity before it cracks, ruptures, and ends…

In the past she would have materialised their encounter, with ink and brush gracefully executed on rice paper. This is her way of control over the unexplained, to catch the lucid but inexplicable moments with lines bold yet fluid, or lightning quick but virile strokes in which strength is paramount. Altogether an exuberant work full of feeling and vigour for her to remember and forget. A snapshot of eternity that puzzles her and makes her blood thicken running dark and magnetic through her limbs to her spine. She felt the weighing shade creeping on the edge of her loins, a dangerous symmetry of fire. *What could it be this time, passion or passing foolishness?* It was difficult to come back.

In the beginning she restricted herself to one visit to him a week. She would cook a meal for them both to share. He dived for lotus roots which she prepared in ten different ways, as a cold dish, hot and spicy, or simmered to be served as porridge, for rice was worth gold and not easy to get hold of. After the meal, as they sat together to have tea, the young stranger would take the brush to write something for her on sheets of fan-shaped paper he had found in the house. She speculated upon the reason why he never spoke to her. She was mute all right but she was not deaf! The truth she had to face soon was chilling, unquestioned and unbreakable.

"You ink like?" One day he wrote the question for her after they finished a late lunch. He had such handwriting, as if the lines came off the paper flying! She never knew this writing before, unbearably light, almost as captivating as his smile which stirred up memories of a diamond-encrusted sea.

He passed the brush to her, which she refused, like other times.

"I made," he continued writing, like other times. Like other times it was an incomplete sentence with words in scrambled order or missing.

She found herself unable to resist the eyes of gilded black. Feverish shadow of a blossom field deep inside him fell without cease, wilted petals raining on a quiet but sad melody.

She lowered her face to think for a minute. This time she decided to take the loaded brush he offered her. Their hands touched, ephemeral hint of the skin. She felt his body quiver, her heart pounding in her mouth. With an effort she glanced down at the table.

"How?" she wrote in a hurry, feeling a little dizzy for a while.

"Lotus roots. Mud. Well." He answered in broken, written words, but she understood him. He mixed the sludge from the lotus pond with water from the draw-well in front of the house.

"It's a magic well," she wrote. "Its name is Wuan: forget me not."

"Make more ink. Dark," she wrote, pondering how many invisible thoughts are thought every day in the world and how many love letters unwritten? How could she explain to him that the scent of the ink intoxicated her? Her sense of smell was very strong, nothing revives the past so completely as a smell once associated with it. How could she explain that his ink smelt the same as her undergarments when she went to bathe the other day? As if she had wet herself like a baby! She breathed in a whiff of jasmine sprinkled on fresh rice soup, sweet balsamic fragrance with a trace of vanilla delicate yet peppery like Kublai Khan's secret garden. The heady symphony of euphoric notes excited her and made her giddy and sedate at the same moment. It's the scent of destiny, it smells so good that it should be bottled by the finest perfumer in the world. She had missed him and enjoyed his absence. How could she explain the missing that is missing? She can't.

She stood up and left.

Next time when she came back, she brought her calligraphy material with her. From now on she would visit the house every day. She would find an excuse to tell her husband, he would let her go because every minute he saw her he was reminded of his son killed brutally together with tens of thousands others. He had died with them ever since. Not a single minute of his life went by without him picturing what his boy went through. He wouldn't cry or speak. There is no grief like tearless grief, no guilt like wordless guilt.

One day, at sundown she burst into the house. Sheng that was not Sheng was surprised. He didn't expect a second visit in one day. He wanted to show her to the writing table and ask but he couldn't move. Glued to the spot, he watched her undressing herself, peeling the thin summer dress off her body. The dress hugged her form, too tight, the fabric had turned stiff after many washings. It feels as if she took off a chimney she had been wearing for ages. Holding her breath, she pulled her white cotton shorts down past her knees, letting it drop to the floor around her ankles. She did it with slow, minimal movement, quietly, without making any sound. Standing in the murky light, naked, her eyes shone with a speckled brilliance to match two small white rice seed pearls in her ears. The twilight shed through the shutters, printing irregular shadows on her flushed skin. She turned in her bare feet to face him, her arms folded under her breasts, quivering, silhouetted against the grey wall – a golden halo. Suddenly, she buried her face in her hands and cried quietly, her shoulders jolting. She reminded him of a dying moth.

He didn't know what to do. Maybe he wanted to hold her, he couldn't be sure of his feeling. The opposite of love is not hate but not feeling, no feeling at all. He would rather be a shoe.

He walked over and picked up the golden kimono at her feet to hand it to her. The silk robe had been lying there all this time, on the same spot where she left it on the day they met. Nobody collected the piece from the floor to store it away. Every time when she left, he would drape the silk around her imaginary body. He saw her drown, swallowed by big, dark waves. He wanted to reach out and save her life. But he was disgusted by himself. His hands had touched death and toyed with it. He was not sure if he killed for a bit of coloured ribbon, for the lies! He couldn't bear to look in her eyes starry with tears. He wanted to tell her that all the arms they needed are for hugging. He wanted to ask her forgiveness.

She took his hand and kissed it. The silk robe flowed through his fingers like strands of lemon sand. He felt his blood rushing, pumping through his body to his head, warm, stinging human blood. He thought he will never feel it again. He believed he had unlearned all good things in life. He felt her heartbeats, as he laved his hand over her soft stomach in her breasts. The touch was enough to make everything waver in front of his eyes. He staggered on his feet, intoxicated with unexpected happiness. Why must happiness feel like physical pain, like suffering? Something collapsed in him, he had to hold onto her – they had to hold onto each other. Like molten iron they crumpled, their bodies squeezing to one shape on the cool flooring, sizzling. The charred despair, flaming burden enveloped in golden light. Outside the windows they heard the lotus field chanting a faraway love song. *Shalalala.*

"Did you love him?" Reigan asks. He is thinking about two quotes he read yesterday in the evening. Checking quotes is what he does when he needs to know if he still can think. One quote says: "Memory is a crazy woman that hoards coloured rags." The other one: "Memory is a child walking along a seashore; you never can tell what small pebble it will pick up and store away among its treasured things." Which is which in this case?

"That was what he asked too," she replies, broodingly. " 'Do you forgive me? Do you love me?' In this same order, written again and again on a fan-shaped sheet after we made love. At first I thought he wanted to apologise for his country and people. Then I realised it's not that. He wanted ME to forgive HIM.'

"He wanted your personal forgiveness. *Why?*"

"I wondered too in the beginning. But – "

"But?"

"I suppose I didn't want to know. I assumed that he felt guilty about my age, his age. It was me who should feel guilty."

"Did you?"

"Never a moment."

"But like you said, you looked young, so young he wouldn't have a clue!"

"It's my curse. An intelligent woman shouldn't look pretty, that's the lesson of life. Life does find out things once in a while. But the thing is, the stranger knew a *lot* about me, perhaps more than I would ever myself. Even before we met we shared secrets that would outshine the most intimate of lovers."

"What secrets?"

"Shame, Doctor. We shared shame inside those grey walls. Soon, I was to learn that the stranger was not who he said he was."

Summer, 1944

Every day she slipped out of her house to meet the young lover. She would seize every chance and tell her husband little lies that came up in her. Not that he cared. Not that she *knew* he would care if he discovered the truth. She didn't. In fact she was so sure he didn't that she wanted to find out. A sick game, she knew.

One day at noon she heard her husband leaving the house. Once a week he would visit the local teahouse at fixed hour. He never said so but it was what men did during these summer hours when one is too drowsy to be alive but too alive to be dead. Even in an isolated village like Wuan where the rules of the outside world still apply. Perhaps it was another way saying: "Forget me not".

After her husband left for pleasure girls, she sneaked into his bedroom upstairs. The gramophone was spinning mutely in the corner, he forgot to turn it off. She took the record and hid it under her arm. She ran, her heart fluttering in her throat like summer wings. Rushing past the yard, she followed the dusty road to a covered pathway. Threading through thistles and fields of dandelions, she walked for a while then disappeared.

From the village, people caught a glimpse of a little girl darting among thistles and dandelion fields, her body floating over the hills like a swallow. Their eyes followed her all the way down to the chasm. Then she disappeared. When she emerged again, they saw her running up the stairs cut by the river in the rocks. As it happened, people believed that they saw a fish instead of a girl. The whisper of the auspicious sign of goldfish emerging from the Yangtze spread quickly. Soon everybody started to believe that the war was near its end.

Short of breath, with the music tucked under her arm, she arrived at the pink-roofed house to find it strangely quiet. She searched around and searched more. She was scared. The idea that he had left forever nearly asphyxiated her. At last, she found the shed behind the shrubbery.

He turned when he heard her footsteps, his face ashen with fright, his body tense and tight. If nerves could snap she would have heard it.

She walked over and smacked his face. She hugged him, so tight she hurt him. She wanted to tell him: "Yes, I love you. Yes, I forgive you whatever it is you've done. Whatever it is you are hiding from me. Because you are my lover, brother and child. You are my child. *Sheng*. Life – "

She saw the revolver in his hand, and all of a sudden, she realised something. The broken sentences he wrote on fanned paper for her. His muteness, he never spoke a word. The young man didn't talk because he could not. *The stranger didn't speak her language!*

Her hand touching to the gun, she read the words cast in the black iron handgrip:

Showa 11th year, Japanese Imperial Army.
Reg. No. XXX XXX

He was not a homeless who lost his family in the war. Or rather she was the one who had wanted it that way, and he merely played along with her. She refused to find out the truth about the stranger. She feared to hear another story that would break her and take away the last ounce of her strength to punish herself! Life became a punishment for her since the day six years ago. Now wake up and count on facts! The young man was not Chinese. Worse. Her lover was a Japanese soldier!

An officer who ran away from battlefield and went into hiding to avoid penalty charge for his desertion? She reasoned hastily.

He placed the loaded weapon in her hand and helped her to point the barrel to his temple.

"Forgive me," he spoke in his mother tongue. He was pale and all in a tremble like a leaf on a cold wintry tree. She pitied him. She thought of the woman who waited somewhere far away for her son to return, who never returned.

In a flash, she decided she is a murderer by choice.

Not lowering the weapon, she backed out, her right arm tense, ready to pull the trigger. She waited a few seconds and aimed again from a distance. Putting out her other hand, slowly she unloaded. She had never touched a gun before!

The zing of the bullet numbed the air. The short-lived whistle bored an ugly hole in seasoned wood. She cried out, casting the smoking gun aside. She dived to his body in a puddle of blood – which appeared to be only a trick of light as she came closer.

She turned his body and looked for a wound. There was no wound. She understood something she hadn't thought about before.

These men are taught to shout "Banzai! May Great Imperial Japan live forever!", in so loud a voice as to scare away the fear which threatened to consume them. But the feel of the cold steel makes them shudder, they can't wait to replace the weapon in the holster and have tea. These men want to live as everybody else. The dark of the night makes them afraid, thought of home brings tears to their eyes, and when enemies are at the gates they shut themselves and pray. *The soldier simply fainted!*

She sat down on the floor. The stranger was real for her now, a human being made of flesh and blood. She waited for the young man to wake and regain consciousness, and if he didn't, she decided, she would wait as long as it took. Ages. Centuries. Millennia.

It was dark outside when he finally woke to the sound of nocturnal birds. She smiled at him and put the music in his hand. The rest of the hours she would let him sing for her. He had a voice sonorous and sweet, with a husky tenderness like actors from movies, so clear that every syllable quivered in the languorous air yet so intimate like rustling sheet between your fingers. He had a voice of velvet.

Black velvet!

> *Summertime*
> *And the livin' is easy*
> *Fish are jumpin'*
>
> *…*

The cracked voice hums the familiar tune to herself, calling Reigan back from the unlikely world where he would rather have stayed forever.

"I didn't know remembrance of happiness could wear one out," she says. "I can't believe the purpose of life is to be happy. I used to think that happiness is a metaphor reserved for writers who have nothing to say."

"You felt happy with him?"

"We ate, copulated and sang. Hours and hours filled with trivia. I would cut his nails and make them really round and smooth, like I did with my little son a long time ago; I loved those tiny round fingers tickling my face. I wanted my lover to copy the touch of a memory. I made Sheng that is not Sheng touch me the same way my dead son did. I made him hugging my legs crying, and the other things a little child would do. But that joy, the sweet and sour glazed sadness and happiness. The thrill I never knew before! I thought I would be punished one day for being so happy."

Weighing up her words, Reigan studies her face intently. He is aware of the obvious guilt trip and empathises with it; it's not his job to judge a patient.

"Perhaps you enjoyed doing something forbidden, something our society is against and would by no means accept?" he volunteers.

"'All men are equal before fish.' My mom said that. Love is its own race."

"Were you not afraid?"

"Of what?"

"Your husband, that he would burst into the house and find you there?"

"I *wish* he had come. But he wouldn't until everything went wrong."

"I brought you new sheets," Reigan says, showing the white linen on the chair back. "You need a hand?"

"I'm all right. I don't want to scare you away with what you shall find under these. We still have a story to finish, Doctor."

She smiles her sybaritic smile.

Honey and wine, Reigan thinks. In the countryside, honey wine is called *medica*. Farmers use it to make skin wounds heal better. The liquor will extract truth from her hearts, lay bare the scars and heal the world.

"It's the song," he says, humming. "*Fish are jumping, the cotton is high*…I don't have velvet, but at least I can offer you cotton sheets for a little cool down. This is probably the worst Indian summer I knew yet. So he sang for you – "

Summer, 1944

The hellish summer season passed without her noticing. In fact the airless weather never ended. *It worked!* she thought. She had wanted that their song would work like a spell, days and years would be put on hold, and they would always love each other inside the grey walls of the house, free from time and space, like a painting. Like a painting!

She believed that the spell had worked when Dog Days slipped quietly into the Indian summer, the worst she knew yet. When she woke up one morning, she had the first attack of headache. She felt queasy. She went to the bathroom and retched something clear and sticky. She looked into the mirror to face herself. She felt ashamed: she was pregnant.

She left for their daily tryst, later than usual, to find him waiting for her at the rocky lookout point. She was angry with him. She had told him not to take any risks. At the base of the towering rock she made love to him. Pebbles creaked under their bodies, sharp edges cutting into their flesh. In the pale sun his shadow stretched falling upon her, looming like a black mountain harbouring hundreds of honeybirds pecking on her cheeks, lips and breasts, drinking from her light chocolate nipples. The mountain trembled, and curved back, like a flame in the wind. *Lower, lower. How low will he go?* Her heart tripped over itself, racing, her entire body tweaked. His hands clutching her buttocks, his impatient tongue dipped into the sugar-rich nectar. She felt her inside burning, a dark red, tongue-shaped fire, hissing, crackling, popping, and every of her inner recesses burnt up, burnt down, wrecked, ravaged by leaping flames that turned her into ruins with no roof left and no shades under the trees for her to hide herself. A place where she would have stayed forever and become part of its eternal imperfection. A roaring lioness perhaps who knows many tricks to amuse herself? But then, the sultry, tremulous flame ceased its quest unexpectedly, abruptly, causing her to almost choke in her yearning for yearnings. Before she could beg him to return to her, to destroy her completely and reduce her to ashes, but beg him to stay just a little while longer, she felt him again, in the folds of her skin, cool as rain, slinky as lynx. Searching curiously, a sika deer is licking water at a melting creek tumbling down her legs...She wanted so badly to be crushed in a tough grip. She wanted him to pull her hair in darkness, in any light after dusk. She felt the tingly, feverish ice in her tightened bones, crushed, her veins slit open and the blood is black. She lifted her body, travelling to him with the agility of a cheetah, grasping his waist with one arm and cradling her neck with the other, her shoulders drawn back. She gave herself to the source of the skies and abyss –

They were slumping, joined by the slides of loose earth and stone along the steep hillside, descending in a hurry to be rolled in rolled out, tumbling over the edge into the deepness of the chasm. They hit the soggy sand bed to soft-land in sweet-green, flowing urgency of river that caught them in huge sheets rushing out eastwards, cleansing blood from their skin –

Some hours later when he brought her back to the house, she wanted him to make love to her again, in the lotus field. He felt something changed in her. He observed the sombre gleam in her eyes and pale cheeks. He couldn't ask. She made him afraid and confused. But he wanted her, now more than ever. Maybe he sensed that something terrible was going to happen, that he was losing her.

He complied.

She let him undress her. He put her in the golden kimono lying there on the same spot. He wrapped her as if she was a precious piece of porcelain, as if it were some ancient, forgotten ritual.

He scooped her from the tatami flooring, her body feathery and warm in his arms. They waded into the sea of giant, inky leaves whispering darkest desire. *Shalalala.*

"Do you have a wife, Doctor Reigan?" she asks, breaking off her story.

"Alice is hot. She's cool."

"Strange."

"What is?"

"Two extremes but they mean the same. Hot and cool, it's like light *de*light. Have you ever been to the sea, Doctor?"

" 'The fishermen know that the sea is dangerous and the storm terrible, but they have never found these dangers sufficient reason for remaining ashore.' Van Gogh," Reigan lectures, "and yet no sea is ever more dangerous than the sea of the mind."

"Then you know the law to control the sea, Doctor?"

"I'm not sure, yet."

"In order to rule the sea, you have to face it. Receive and not take, let it be the sea it wants to be, boiling over bubbling up. You hoist the sail to ride the dangerous waves. You pass cities on the horizon, unfamiliar faces draw close, you feel their pain because you know yours. Any minute life could end, you could drown, the faces you knew will vanish as if they never existed. *Puff!* Gone, like blowing out a candle. Only when you realise this, not only realise but bear it in your heart like a diamond, then you can face the sea without hurting yourself.'

"Tell me about your sea, Butterfly."

"My sea – "

He waded into the sea of giant, inky leaves, murky water clouded around his young shoulder. He held her in his arms, as if it were some ancient, forgotten ritual. They disappeared from the eye of the world. The world disappeared to them.

She had him take her violently, had him unleash all that power, her nails planting in his skin, impaling him. She sobbed, her eyes burning with pain and pleasure, her fingers tangled themselves in his hair. She wanted to let go: she wanted to stay.

He watched her choke, her body tensing in his arms. He didn't stop making love to her. Black mud buried her face, engulfing her breasts and her dazzling thighs, sucking her down. Slowly, she sank to the swamps of shadows, taking him with her to the ocean of forgetfulness.

He didn't stop making love to her.

Quietly, almost unobserved, like some organism from the deep ocean that only blooms at night, the golden silk unfurled around the pale oval of her face, stunningly beautiful, fading. But then, in the blink of an eye, he saw, just like that, he saw from unintelligible depths, a speckled light rising to him. A ginger moon, augmenting, throwing patches of flaked shadows over her milky skin re-emerging. At the centre of the blissful stars, an elegant twirl took shape. Flitting wings beating past his face. He felt his body lift, intangible as cloud, bounded by peace like peace of mind. He chased after her into the soot-black mire, which, to his astonishment, was no longer dense. A myriad of shiny little blades blinding him.

Many days later when he tried to understand what exactly had happened, he would remember his visit to a temple near Kyoto some years ago.

Before he left home for China, he went to the large temple complex to pray for safe return. On his way out he passed the dewpond to find a goldfish swimming alone in fresh rain water. He came closer to have a better look at it, and he was stunned. As if it was made of colourless wax, its entire body was transparent, showing the tiny little heart beating inside. He didn't know why he was moved to tears. The next day he boarded the military vessel to fight a war in a far country.

And yet his remembrance didn't help him answer his questions. He had gone to extreme lengths to put together the jigsaw puzzle of that particular day. It could have been a dream. The only picture he recalled was an ocean of translucent, soot-black ink where they swam together. They had transformed into two golden butterflies with tantalising wings sailing in eternity, as if they became a painting.

"That's how you became aware of your – let's say – natural power?" Reigan asks.

"I would rather say it's fate."

"Fate, huh?"

"Yes, it is the doing of the unscientific engineer called Fate that I turned up in this sickroom after decades living in the shadows of the condemned."

"This is the place where the lovers met, didn't you? The pink-roofed house once stood here – "

"We made love on that floor under your feet."

She raises an arousing finger.

"What happened to the house?"

"The war ended in 1945. The war followed by the civil war which lasted for another four years. Communists fighting

Nationalists. During that time, the house served as a military infirmary. Then someone came up with the idea to build a real hospital. They decided to get rid of the old bit."

"But one part was kept for a reason. This room even survived the Cultural Revolution!"

"Doctor, don't you ask yourself why I don't die of thirst? You brought me food. I *love* beef! Thanks. But you forgot about drink!'

"The well, of course!" Reigan affirms on a snap of fingers.

"You are an unriddler, Doctor. Next time I'll let you do my Sudoku."

"I'm number dyslectic, I always get less paid than I'm worth. But I guess it's OK, I do what I love to do."

"It is indeed the magic well after which the village is named. Wuan: *forget me not*. And I believe that the architect considered carefully the Feng Shui principles in his design of the hospital. Feng and Shui, wind and water. Here on these hills he didn't need to worry about wind. However, in order to keep the energy flowing in a full circle, he kept the old well which he cleverly masked by way of a brilliant construction – "

"I suppose water and the mind pretty much work the same way. Any sort of block-up would damage the flow, then you drown."

"Do you feel drowned at all, Doctor? Since this place is completely under water."

"What? You mean right now?"

"Right now, right then, right this moment."

"What do you mean? But I don't understand – "

"You will. Right answers wait for the right moment."

They both fall silent for a moment, subdued by a sense of wonder as they listen to the lotus field brought to a whisper on a puff of wind. Through the small vent up the wall Reigan smells ripe summer berries from the woods, he craves a soul-stirring ice cream.

"Can you tell me more about that day? Your magic?" he says.

"Magic the logic, the responsibility of a good story," she grins. "Once I heard that love can sometimes be magic but magic can sometimes just be an illusion. I think I can live with that. That said, I can tell you what I can tell you, although words elude me to capture the exact occurrence or it be by grace of fabulous lunacy! It is not that I don't know. I know perfectly well what the answer is. It's the question I seek. It has always been questions that we sacrifice for an unsatisfying answer. I remember we played games like children do. We played sailboats in an inky ocean of inky waves. You remember Columbus crossing the seas, Doctor? It was such a ship, ancient, with a female figure on the front, her hair tousling around her face, her dress lifting in the air. We sailed in the womb of the sea, new, spotless, innocent. He was my captain, I was his ship. He decked me with sweet-scented flowers. Like an angel maiden I floated. I wished we never arrived and the word shore never pronounced. But then, all of a sudden, I found myself sitting on the edge of the well and he was washing me. He was rinsing me with cool water from a gourd spoon, I felt happy like a fish. I put out a finger to write in the black mud on his body. *yumeji ni wa / ashi mo yasumezu / kayoedomo/ utsutsu ni hitome / mishigoto wa arazu…* "

"What does it mean?"

"It's a Japanese poem he taught me. It's a Tanka. *I go often to you in my dreams, along dream paths, but I never see you in the real world.* At this point he stood up and went into the kitchen. When he came back, he brought along a writing brush. He asked me to write the lines on his body. Actually he said "engrave" – "Please engrave". It's one of the phrases I picked up during the months. But then, once I started writing, I saw ruby beads swelling up on his skin. More blood rushing off his back and shoulders where my writing hand left traces, mingled with large, salty sweatdrops. I understood he had tied a little razor inside the brush head! But my hand wouldn't stop, and I kept carving in his young torso covered in a crisscross of miniature rivers of crimson trailing off in all directions, drawing out the cruel, secret landscape of our love. A sensation of warmth filled my heart, making it ache making it beat, a powerful bass drum of Death –

"My stomach growing lighter, my hand kept writing, the hidden, sharp blade kept piercing in his flesh and skin, and my eyes kept locked on the dark, almond shapes of his eyes twisted by shots of tender spasm. Running my hand through his hair soaked with tears and body juices, I was bent suckling cruelly on his wounds like a hungry infant. Such a sweet pain I couldn't stand! Such a bitter pain he will never forget! I want to heal him – I want to heal myself. My tongue stabbing and penetrating the wounds where the skin is broken, I wanted to free us from a past.

"My lips left their shapes covering his fluorescent chest, his throbbing neck, his forehead too young to be in love. I covered him with shattered rose petals and perfect strawberry of my bloody kisses. Countless bleeding little hearts. Then I opened his curled fingers for him and cut into his palm: EAT ME. I felt his teeth burning in my thighs with unfathomable delight and misery – "

Nurse Lyn is enjoying music, her shoulders swaying to the beat coming through her headphones.

Last time Reigan agreed that she may turn on the speaker boxes once in a while. "It's for my poor little fish, Doctor Reigan. I'm afraid it's dying," she had begged him.

Through the thin glass wall, Reigan saw the creature tilt around water, inexpertly moving, casting a florid, fancy shadow on the white wall. When he took a second look, he was shocked to find the snow-white fantail tainted by a sick grey-green, trailing droopily behind the semi-transparent body that ballooned like a puffy swollen eye after some heartbroken tears.

"If you keep it down. Once a day, maximum," Reigan gave her the go ahead in a sentimental mood.

He pokes his head around the door and says in a loud voice, "Put it on, Lyn!"

"*What?*"

"Music!" Reigan makes a gesture for her to take off her headphones. "I want to hear fish requiem at least once in my life. *Momento mori* in D minor."

A quirky, passionate female vocal suddenly explodes out of the mini boxes on her desk. The clamorous, booming sound carries into the empty corridor and sickbay:

> *In Malta, catch a swallow,*
> *For all of the guilty, to let them free.*
> *Wings fill the window,*
> *And they beat and bleed*

"OK, found it, ice on Mars!" The nurse clicks the mouse to turn off the volume on her computer. "Please don't fire me,

Dr. Rei *Gun*. It won't happen again, I promise. Kate Bush is a dish, my kind of babooshka. Oh heavenly *gesundheit*, have you seen that?"

Running to the window, the nurse points her hand to the last yellow light receding on the leaden horizon. A toothed line glints through the closing clouds, doomfully dramatising the faint sound of thunders as if someone were tearing silk fans in heaven.

"Don't threaten me with love, baby. Let's just go walking in the rain. Yeah!" she yells, excited.

"Love was in the newspaper last week and the week before. Love is old news. We live in a country where you can choose between old news and good news," Reigan laments scornfully.

"But look at the birds! It's for real now. *When the birdie flies low, touching water with her wing, it's gonna rain.* My girlfriend taught me the lullaby her grandma taught her mother. She says these are the songs the earth has grown old with. The typhoon is coming, you can smell it in the air." She takes a deep breath.

"How are the patients today? Improving?"

"On the road to victory I would say. The girl is checking out. Yesterday she asked her mother to buy her a new fairy nightlight, a merry-go-round with goldfish in it. Can you believe it? It' s like a spell or something. All of a sudden it's over, and everybody simply stopped vomiting as if it's a decision made by the central government. When I checked in today, the patients were arguing whether it was a goldfish or a little girl running up the bend of the Yangtze river."

"What are you talking about?"

"You mean you don't know? CNTV Breakfast News. I swear I have never seen such a weird thing in my life –
Dr. Reigan, are you all right?"
Reigan can hardly breathe, cringing from an ash-coloured heaviness in his chest which he has been experiencing for some weeks now. In the region of his eye sockets he senses the burning tentacles spread out, the mysterious throbbing pain that seems a symmetry of pain and pleasure, and the unbearable light as if his skull is turning into one big light bulb so brilliant that he fears the rest of him would fade to a shadow.

"Something is gonna happen," he mumbles, barely holding the ground.

"What?"

"Nothing. I will be in my office."

Gulping a lungful and holding it, Reigan dashes off in a sprint, not keen to throw up in front of the young woman; it would look like showing an opinion.

Kicking the door shut, he runs for the desk to grab the bin to make a few disgusting sounds. No substantial portion. But then, his eyes fall on a tiny square shape on the off-white linoleum floor. He nips the brown yellow tablet between his two fingers. This is insane but the numbers on it don't lie. 0406. It is the pharmaceutical ID number for Pimozide, a drug to treat delusional disorder. Cold moisture stands out on his forehead. In his ears he hears a squeaking little voice:

Which one, Dr. Reigan, the reality of the lozenge, or the one the lozenge seeks to confine in its well-meant, well-measured insipidness?

An acute ache in his abdomen weighing him down, Reigan drops to the floor, his hand reaching for the glass of water on the edge of his desk. He counts to five, and fires the dose to the bin –

Hit!

"He is coming, isn't he? You are waiting for him to show up in this room! *Who is he, Sheng that is not Sheng?*"

Reigan bends toward the silhouette shown through the halo. The gilded gingery blush seems to fade a few degrees of strength each time he comes to visit. Her face, however, becomes more luminescent. She is glowing, and incredibly fragile, like a phantasm. Like a dying star!

"We are running out of time," she says in a calm voice, the little mark shy in the corner of her mouth.

Reigan takes a seat on the chair.

"Carry on, please."

Summer, 1944

Each time it took the two of them more courage to say hello goodbye. She didn't know why she went back to her husband, but that was the way to keep the lovers out of trouble. She couldn't have stayed with the young man either. Maybe this thing going on between them meant nothing, she only used him to forget her pain. In fact, she might one day decide never to come back again and stop seeing him all together, just like that, on a whim. She didn't tell him she was with child; she was not sure she would. After all they were strangers.

She needs to think, alone.

She needs a plan.

She has a plan.

She entered the house and went straight to the table where he was waiting for her.

"Loaches," she wrote.

Since her pregnancy she grew an appetite for the raw fish he prepared for her. Her gluttonous desire seemed boundless and beyond any rule. Little bars of chocolate he had saved from his army ration, stolen pickles, wild mushrooms; simmered sweet lotus was her favourite, however. He never dared to ask. He never dared to know. And now she wanted loaches freshly caught in the river.

She showed him a safe path to the shore. As soon as he disappeared from eyeshot, she made a roundabout to the back of the house. She had been walking around with the idea for quite a while. Today she sent him away to find out.

The shed was unlocked. Since she almost killed him last time, she didn't come back here again. She knew something was hidden in the place, besides a gun. She wanted to find out more about the young soldier, a glimpse of a past, a name.

The revolver had disappeared. She searched on the ledge, among the rusty tools where she left it. She looked everywhere for the weapon and sniffed in the thin dust she stirred up like a puppy. It was gone, vanished without a trace. Behind the coal pile she came across a pair of army boots tied together by their shoestrings. She took them in her hands.

The leather was worn, covered in dried mud and dark stains. *Blood.* She unlaced and put into a hand to feel about the shaft. Both shoes were empty. She overturned them to give them a good shake. The cotton insole slipped out, untethering a great snowflake, wafting, which she caught. It was a shred of rice paper, supreme quality, the sort of paper she would work with.

She turned the paper face up. She nearly screamed. Flagging, her legs giving, she crumpled to her knees on the cold floor. A white hot pain pulsing at her temple, blood drumming in her ears. She felt sick. She felt she would *die* this instant. Minutes passed that seemed ages, she didn't have the guts to look in her chilled fist.

After a long agonising wait, at last she held the charred piece of paper to her eye. Something in her still hoped that it was not true, that it was a lie. Yet she was not able to wish that the opposite had not occurred! From the familiar sliver of rice paper, the red little heart stared back at her, shattering her last hopes. Silent sobbings filled up her throat, persistent, lapsing to ragged wailings like an abandoned baby seal on the beach, dying but in disbelief that such a thing as death existed to pardon its suffering.

It was her secret. Instead of using a stone cachet with her name carved on it as an artist's signature, she would autograph her work with her lips coloured in cinnabar red ink. After finishing the scroll, she would complete the artwork with a kiss in the edge. She imagined that a thousand years later when everything was gone, cities wiped out by wars and the last humans barely surviving, the scarlet little heart shape made with her lips will still be saluting the world in ruins.

Suddenly, it occurred to her that more than once he would store away a teacup. He didn't allow her to wash it, arguing that her heart will still be with him when she left, and he will be kissing her; kissing the cordate, rouge shade left on the brim. He only wanted to make sure that the shape match the one hidden in his shoe! His pitiable glances, his guilt-ridden, muffled crying as she watched him sleep, he grinds the broken flow of words, "Forgive me, will you forgive me".

The man is the murderer of her son!

She held the scroll she sent Sheng away with six years ago. This is the last of it, burnt, stinking of death! The murderer tracked down the farthest point to find the woman who made the heart on the scalded paper. When he did, he drew out his plan carefully. He lured her with birdsong to the abandoned house only to ask her forgiveness, because the coward didn't have the courage to kill himself! Then blind fate cast off her veil, they became lovers. Now she was carrying his child!

She didn't know for how long she had been lying there, feeling her guts washed up alongside her, hollow, dead. A voice in her head said: "Stand up, woman. Stand up and do it!"

She held herself up, with strength that surprised her. She got to her knees and steadied on her feet. In a split second she inventoried the to-do list, in chronological order.

She wants to know how her son died.

She wants to know why he died, why anyone.

She wants to pull that trigger.

There is no gun.

When he came in, she was waiting, seated in the bare room, a vast, clear space filled with the crisscross of looming shadows behind her back. She didn't turn.

He put away the dripping creel, walked over to the low table and sat down facing her. She had changed into the golden silk kimono, gathered fabric wound around her body like a snake, her straight dark hair clung to her face, sallow and cold. She reminded him of the lady from a Japanese ghost story that scared him as a child. He reached out to part her hair from her eyes, and touched her mouth. She jolted. His head lowered a fraction to discover the knife clutched in her hand, her other hand folded open showing a charred corner of paper. The red little heart met his eyes. *She knew.*

He had been waiting for this moment for years now, ever since the day he decided to find the woman who will kill him. He had never expected himself to be so calm.

He laid out both his arms on the tabletop and rested his head between them. His nape showed, young, vulnerable, and throbbing. He turned to look at her. He wanted to see her when he died, see her tender hand that he loved, the hand that gave the right amount of pleasure...

The metal glinted in the gloom, faltering white light. He read the words engraved in the blade, syllable by syllable, letter by letter, with a mute voice dragging long and low like monks' prayer at a funeral:

ZWIL—LING—J—A—HENC—K—E—L—S—Com—Company—

The twin figures dancing. He closed his eyes –

A dull, grim sound rebounding through his head. Cold air touching his cheek, under his feet the ground quaking. He wondered if it was his head, cut off, landing on the floor, rolling gravely away from his body. He didn't feel pain. Death doesn't feel so awful after all.

He opened his eyes to smile at her. There was neither defiance nor hypocrisy in that smile. A smile that travelled over her mind: a human face. The head rolled on the table. He looked at the knife planted between his spread arms. *She had killed his shadow lying large across the table!*

She had killed without killing! She won from the mad game without winner, from hate without cause. She slit the throat of a pack of old lies.

She won from herself!

His eyes following her hand pulling out the knife. The sharp touched the back of his hand, the blade sank deep into his skin. A rush of blood crept away, drawing warm, beet-coloured roots between his fingers, feeding their longings and grief. The incised, split edge lengthening, the singular line closed. A ruby heart took shape in his flesh.

She leaned over. She rubbed her trembling lips against his blood-soaked, wounded hand, tracing his arm, shoulders and neck, printing there countless strawberry hearts. She moved closer to him so he could read her distorted mouth.

"Fuck me," she breathed in his ear.

He scooped her from the tatami flooring, her body feathery and warm in his arms. He waded through the breathing space of freedom, holding her close to him, as if it were some ancient, forgotten ritual. They disappeared from the eye of the world; the world disappeared to them.

He put her down gently, across his lap, un-sashing the costly piece of silk. He watched the lining unfurl around her milky skin, subtle embroidery of hundreds of flowery petals flit, fly, float, sunset snow. For a while he remained unmoving, gazing at her. She looked so pure, unsullied, like an angel maiden he didn't dare to touch. His mind drifted to the snow field in Kyoto where he once saw a fisherman fishing. The man pulled in the lines out of a hole in the frozen dewpond. The little fish struggled with twisting fins, and almost instantly, the tiny body was arrested in a frost crescent on silver blue ice. For the first time he felt the amazing sensation, a numbed flame churning from his pancreas until every of his pores was filled with a fiery sedation, burning! burning! burning! (A sensation which he many years later would try in vain to find with girls of his age.) At that moment a young fox emerged from piled snow, crippled, white fur flecked with dirt. The fisher shooed it away. He had wanted to chase after it. He had wanted to hug the hungry weak little thing, feed it and take care of it until it cried from healing pain.

"*Kitsune,*" he whispered, touching his lips to her mouth corner. He kissed the blushing little mark not too high and not too low, not too big and not too small. An imperfection exactly right. He pulled the creel to him, emptying the loaches jumping alive to cover her hair, her eyes, her soft stomach and ankles. Gently he cradled her body with his. He had captured more than her body, he cradled her heart in his young hands. *My little white kitsune.*

He loved her with all his tears and sweet-scented juices draping from her throat to her collar bones and chest to become a long pearly necklace. He wished that their ocean was never to end and the word shore never pronounced. He pushed slowly inside her.

...

Some hours later, a man stood on the hilltop. He looked at a shadow in the distance. Along the river bend she walked, her steps so light as if treading on sunburnt clouds, inspiring a swift arc of birds soaring to a jade-green evening sky. His eyes followed the tableaux until the fringed silhouette submerged to the day's end. He turned walking down the dusty road at a sedate pace, passing the yard, climbing the stairs to his bedroom to wait for his wife. She should arrive any moment. He had a present for her.

He fumbled for a record, which he put on the gramophone. By now he had discovered that his wife was a thief. At first he believed it was part of her follies, her secret writing, her petty lies. She would steal his music records and return them a few days later. Then there were the ones which she never brought back home. His speculations left many questions unanswered. One day, he followed her to a house deep in the woods…

A harsh *chewking* sound attracted his attention. He ambled off to the birdcage hung in the window. Pouring some water in the saucer, he stared for a while at the grey wings beating helplessly behind the bars. *Would a drowning human look the same?* He bought the mockingbird for his wife's birthday. When she was a child, his wife paid daily visit to a bird collector with her aunt. However, when her aunt didn't show up one day, they told the girl that her aunt had left them. Years later, his wife learned about the truth. "It's a family tradition to punish the adulteress and her lover this way," his wife had told him. "So they threw them into the river. The lovers were drowned together."

I am a man of tradition, he thought. From the window he saw his wife arrive in the yard.

Part II. Chasing butterfly: Confessions of a murderer

man walks up the boulevard separating the trendy district in two areas, Kita to the North and Minami to the South. It's a sunny day in Aoyama, Tokyo. The bent road calls to his mind a river from long ago and far away.

He is fond of the part of the city he visits regularly, its bustling quarters with jazz clubs (The Blue Note for one), bookshops, and the handsome youth he studies from a distance. Would they hum the haunting song in their dreams, like he does, night after night, seventy years long? How many days will still be left for him to sing, he wonders. He is venerable, like they say. *How many days will still be left for him to finish his story?* There are so many great ways to tell a story, and every way is tailored to the body and soul –

He halts abruptly to look into the parcel he clutches in his hand, his knuckles white. Wrapped in an old newspaper, the bound, fan-shaped sheets are covered with ink marks only he could decipher. It's his private handwriting. Once upon a time he aspired to become a writer, perhaps this is another reason why he likes to be here. This is the place where a range of writers (Murakami-san, for instance) call home, and where many a masterpiece of literature was penned and is being penned this very moment. It's time to tear wounds from his guts and tell the story that has no end marks. A period, question mark, or exclamation point? It is such a well-kept secret even for the lovers. Now he has to clap the net over the butterfly of the moment, before the moment passes and his life is gone! He settles on a plan, heading for his scheduled destination, the cemetery.

The Aoyama Reien from the Meiji era is held by Tokyoites to be the most beautiful spot of the capital. In daylight hours, traces of incense from the burial ground lends a benign, impenetrable look to the colossal glass buildings lining up the streets, harmoniously mingling with the pale scent of flowers and hushed aromas of fresh pastry. Visitors to the graveyard would notice an old man of measured gait and unflustered guise taking to a quiet corner. For a few minutes he would sit still, lost in a remote ocean of memories. People assume he is talking to the dead, and if they could have heard his mind, they would catch these lines cited over and over. *Ce toit tranquille, où marchent des colombes, entre les pins palpite, entre les tombes; Midi le juste y compose de feux. La mer, la mer, toujours recommencee...*the sea in flames, that sea forever starting and re-starting. They watch him pull out a new sheet of paper. The rest of the day he shall not hear black crows cry, his pen scratching away on the grainy surface. He likes the fan shape of paper of his choice. It helps him remember that any storm in the world will pass, damp typhoon, destructive hurricane, cosmic cyclone, any brouhaha in the pantheon of weather, except a tickling summer breeze of memory that enters his heart like a billowing smooth waltz and tears it apart –

Along the Aoyama-tori boulevard, the man continues his walk on the paved, curved sidewalk. He searches through his memory, like someone holding a homesick camera. 1944, one year before the war ended. Summertime. China. Long shot. A silvery bending arm of water hugging far blue hills, soothing sound of birds *chjjjj*-ing raspy songs of forever. The wide-angle lens of his mind establishing, his eye is led shrewdly to a point blurry at first. And zooming in, the lotus field rolls open in an extra-wide panoramic view of heavy, rubescent blooms brandishing in a sea of giant inky leaves. *Shalalala*. Then, just like a thought, it lights up among a whiff of green leaves: the pink shade of roof –

Brusquely, the harsh sound of siren barges in, interrupting his mental cinema. Forging ahead, an ambulance turns the curve, tearing across the river of heavy day-time traffic. Approaching the zebra crossing, the man advances toward the empty void ahead of him, moving his steps to a different, solid beat. Spellbound, he *can't* stop. He just can't stop.

"Mermaid! A mermaid song! She's calling me home for sashimi…" His trembling lips let go a preoccupied murmur.

The smell of smoking tyres keeps him conscious for a few more seconds, as the screeching sound on asphalt unshackles him from his trance.

Whispers. He heeds a voice drawing close from ages away. Suddenly, it enters his ears:

"Is anyone there? Can you hear me?"

He moans, and slowly opens his eyes to see two faces bending over him.

"You are fine, Ojiisan. Welcome back!"

The young man in a long white jacket gives him an efficient smile, drawing his fingers from the patient's pulse to take notes in his health record. The doctor turns his attention to the nurse and says:

"Lyn, keep a close eye on him. *I don't believe in miracles.* I mean, just how many people get hit by an ambulance and come out in one piece!"

"I think I'm lucky, Doctor," the patient replies in a blameworthy voice.

"Because you are, Ojiisan!"

Laughing in a hushed, fascinated way, the nurse studies his face with a pair of sharp eyes. She casts him a glance that indelibly burns a fourth-degree scar into his soul.

"They told me that you were hauled up into the air like the flying Dutchman. But look at you, no bruise, no scratch, flawless as a newborn! You are perfectly real, even without miracle. Come on, let's get higher!" Arranging a nest of pillows behind him, she offers her slender arms to help him sit up in bed.

"Please, Doctor. When may I check out?"

Hurrying to the door, the young man stops in mid-step and turns around. He looks at his wristwatch then back at the nurse. "Thursday, Lyn. If the patient is sweet. Tell me, Ojiisan. We have enough madmen running around. What were you thinking when you walked head-on into a moving ambulance?"

"Greek mythology, Doctor?" the patient answers matter-of-factly. "You see, I *must* listen, for siren is a deadly charmer!"

His brows knitted together in confusion, the doctor jots down few more lines in his health record.

Senile dementia, the patient reads his pirouetting pen top. Now the diagnose is official and everybody is satisfied, let's get on with it. He waits until the sound of footsteps fade in the corridor, heading for next round of pulse, stethoscope on chest, tapping abdomen to finally conclude with something ad rectum if one is lucky. Then he raises a low, urgent voice.

"Sumimasen ga, kangoshi-san?" *Nurse, please?*

The red leather shoes move swiftly back to his bedside, the heels ticking pleasantly on the off-white linoleum.

"How can I help you?"

"My book. I always carry it around with me. This may sound daft to you, but all the answers..."

The patient moves suddenly, coughing, seized by a sudden pang of pain in his chest.

"Here it is. You call this a book, Ojiisan?" Reaching in her side-pocket, the nurse extracts a parcel wrapped in old newspaper to hand it to him. "Oh wow, is that a tattoo?" She touches an inquisitive finger to the distinct strawberry shape on the back of his outstretched hand.

"Fairy drawing," he answers, moving away quickly before she can ask another question. He opens the newspaper wrapping and there...

The nurse nods sagely.

"That must be fairy handwriting then," she says, gesticulating to wavy inky lines crawling all over the aged little fans tied together with a blue silk ribbon.

"Which language?"

"*Fish*," he answers again in his succinct voice. Obliged by her searching eyes, he explains himself: "English, Spanish, Finnish, this is Fish. I learned it from a goldfish a long time ago."

"You are a funny old man. I'll check back in a few hours. Don't get yourself in trouble until then, Ojiisan. "

He follows her shoes into the gloom. The sleek red shine of leather dissolves all the way up to the bend in the corridor. The hospital is unlikely quiet, there are no other patients around. Perfect. Secrecy is exactly what a criminal needed; he has to do it right. It strikes him as odd though that no-one has questioned his assumed identity.

He smoothes the streak of silk binding, adjusting the butterfly knot. The blue colour is a footnote to a long, long river, a gentle reminder of the distance between two hearts. Now the time has come finally for the lovers to break the intangible wall from the past. The sheets are somewhat curled, mottled of time. The secret writing on the stained surfaces is the only way through which he can feel her – through an interminable thread of ink. Time was when he and love were acquainted, love showed him a side of itself which leaves him with nothing more to say. Love, like a virgin sheet of paper, is more real than marred feelings printed in books. He runs a quivering finger on the cover page, accurately cracking the hidden message of the warped ink marks. Too easy. Heavily stylised calligraphy shows three English words. It says: "My name is … …" He removes the fountain pen attached to the blue ribbon, unscrews the cap and fills in the ellipses: Maru.

My name is Maru. I am a murderer.

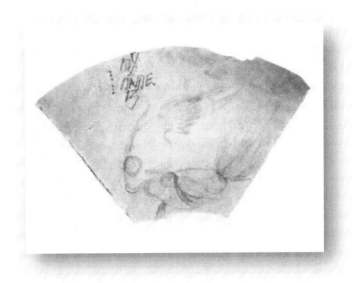

... he fills in the ellipses: Maru. My name is Maru.

His old eyes clouded with moist, he turns the large diamond shape of paper, and starts to read the 68-page indictment against himself, written by himself.

My name is Maru. I was born in Taisho the 9th year, 1920 by Western calendar, in Kyoto, Japan's old capital.

In March of this year, prices collapsed, presaging the beginning of a long-term economic crisis. It was "Crossing the Rubicon" – a point of no return – as would be epitomized by the later historians. The winter had ended as anticipated. The sun passed the equator, the sap flowed in the trees again and the buds began to show up. The animals left their hibernating spot, and soon people started to look in the shades for the first dancing and mating cranes without knowing that our country was heading towards one of the greatest disasters of the 20th century.

Of course, none of these occurrences affected me. Neither did the fact that I had lost my mother to a cradle fever as a result of giving birth. I have a clear image of her though, her dark and beautiful face that bent over me as she breastfed. She had large brown eyes and a lovely voice. Later on people would tell me that I have inherited her eyes and voice.

Since the day I was born I was pampered like a little prince, passed around from arms to arms of our maids who treated me like a costly, sweet pumpkin. Now I think they pitied me for being motherless. I recall myself being so spoilt by the women that I never truly realised I didn't have a mother.

For my father it was a different matter, or so I assumed. As I grew older, I would get to know him better. He was a quiet, reclusive person who talked very little, and when he did, it was always about my upbringing, a subject he often discussed at our dinner table with our family friends who were doctors and educators. I eavesdropped on some of their conversations, and so I learned that my father was worried about me. He was afraid that the maids didn't rear me in a proper way, that I would grow up, not a real man but some dreamy milksop. I never heard him talk about my mother. I didn't know he had a passion, until he took me on one of his mysterious trips in 1927.

The year was committed to memory due to a chain of events. In the spring, the banking system collapsed throughout the country, whereupon General Tanaka Guchi of Seiyukai Party entered politics. General Tanaka became our prime minister. He was a picturesque, opinionated, vigorous man of the sword who came from the Army, where he cut a well-loved and folkloric figure among the crowd of supporters. One year after his inauguration, Japan's population grew to sixty-five million, a fact considered as a good sign by general sentiment, and the faith-winning triumph of our new government. Our people started to believe in the necessity of a military regime. The spirited, belligerent leadership they trusted to be the solution and cure against panic caused by nationwide bankruptcy. I remember it was about this time that patriots and army men started to gather at my father's dinner table. Still three years later, in September 1931, the Japanese Imperial Army would provoke an incident and invade Manchuria without consulting the parliament. But this is for later.

On the 5th of May, my father woke me in the early hours. It was *kodomo no niche*, Boys' Day. Families that have sons should raise carp-shaped banners; carp because of the Chinese legend of a carp that swam upstream and became a dragon. On this day, boys of my country would be found parading in *kabuto*, the traditional Japanese military helmet. From the cradle to the grave we are indoctrinated with the idea that if a man wants to appear strong and healthy, he has to show it fighting. We are brought up with the notion that *otoko no hito* – a real bruiser and hero – is our only option, that war is the only place for us to be. We accept that our country and our emperor are worth more than any of us. Such is how individual lives are reduced to a goose egg, cunningly, in a jolly festive mood.

Kodomo no nichi is also the celebration of the beginning of summer. In the morning my father and I boarded the train to a famous spa in the southern hills. It was the first time I rode a train, I was extremely excited. *Dodeskaden, dodeskaden, dodeskaden,* I went over and over the round of silly words until I practically lost my voice. My father seemed to find himself in the same bouncy, bubbly mood, since he was, contrary to his nature, very talkative. He answered my questions, even the nosy ones. Shortly I was to find out that we were on our way to his mistress whom he had been seeing since my mother's death.

All the way down to the South, I couldn't take my eyes off the ever-changing sceneries flying by outside the window. Mountain crests of all tints of green, pink, and white blossom, theatre of daubs, flecks and patches festooned with carp-shaped flags blowing in the wind. An astonishing sight, as if the fish were alive and gracefully swimming to jump out of the blue of the sky. I fancied that in a few hours I would go for a dip in the *onsen* myself, my body enveloped in nebulous, indigo warmth of the bath. Ever since then I have loved my country for her feminine sensuality attributed to the landscape I remember from the childhood trip. A lucent sense of beauty, limpid and yet cruel to the eye, like a drop of blood from wounded, ruby lips falling on white snow with such precision and perfection that you suddenly can feel it in your mind.

"Who are we visiting, *otoosan*?" I ventured, finding time to sit down at last. I was thrilled by my father's lack of clarity despite his chatty, easygoing appearance.

"Madame K. owns an inn," my father answered. "She has a daughter. How old would Musume-san be, I wonder – "

Musume-san, that was what we called her. *Girl*. I never found out her real name.

"Catch up, boy."

My father gathered our suitcase from the luggage rack.

The road to the inn was stony and full of bumps and holes. The cart we took was primitive, and so uncomfortable that for a moment I worried my head would jump off my body and my body off my feet. As it turned out, we arrived within an hour, safe and sound. The matchless beauty of surrounding views once again distracted me from my torture and made me forget my sore bottom.

Madame K. stood on the hillside waiting for us. In her hand she held two dark blue sets of *yukata* bathrobes with bits of billowing sashes. I don't know what it was. In the blinding sunshine of early summer, that boy that was me foresaw my life was going to change forever and nothing would ever be the same again. In the bright and breezy images I saw a brilliant shadow of great expectations.

"*Yokatta!* How nice of you to have brought your son with you!"

Madame K. greeted us with an elegant bow.

"Musume-san will be very happy to see him. This way, please."

She took my father's suitcase, and we followed her into a huge tatami room where lunch was already being served. We had *miso*, rice bowl and rolled omelette. During our meal Madame K. complained about her business.

"We have received fewer guests than last year. The season has yet to start, but I'm not as optimistic as the newspapers want us to be. I should have faith in General Tanaka and our new government. I do, I really do. Still, despite all the promises they have made us, our lives are obviously getting worse every day."

She spoke in a voice typical of Japanese women, with long-drawn-out syllables as if singing an ever-present elegy.

"Actually, I have been thinking new plans for a while…"

"New plans?" my father enquired.

"Musume-san and I had some discussions the other day. I think I know my decision. I wanted to sell this place anyway and go somewhere else. Now my fear is gone. I will take the girl with me."

"Where are you going?"

"China, perhaps," she sighed, deep in thought. "If we believe what they tell us, Manchuria is our new hope, isn't it?"

"Are you sure? It seems a big thing. Manchuria is a big thing…"

"I shouldn't bother you with my problems," she apologised. Bowing her head, she stood up.

"Please come to bath. I'll wash your back. After that you can do what you came for."

I was wondering what she meant by that, but she was already leaving.

"Don't forget to take your son," she gestured to the two sets of bathrobes she left at the sliding door. "I think he is going to like it. Our onsen is the best in this season!"

And she was right! As a matter of fact I was never going to see such splendid water again in my life, so soft and so smooth that it feels like a thousand kisses deep, a thousand kisses on my skin. A life-giving pain. *She.*

The pool was fenced in by a thin wall made of flat timber to create some illusion of privacy. Through splits and holes I could look out over the soft carpet hills to the ancient, little villages. Monotonous spots of people and farm animals moving in the shadows of spun sugar clouds travelling peaceful and still to the point where the sky and the earth are one. I wondered if the world ended there, if it's always raining at the end of the world for the rainbow to be born. Not that I was wondering too much. While pretending to indulge myself in the bucolic views, I followed Madame K. in the corner of my eye as she moved across the water, her body shimmering with liquid light. She washed my father in the shelter of his arms, giggling like a little girl. They tolerated my presence. I suppose they thought I was too young to know anything. What they didn't realise is the effect they had on me, and the interest I took in them was both absurd and frightening, yet completely natural. I blame it on my childhood. Growing up motherless, women is not a fact of life that can be taken for granted but an enigma wrapped up in a mystery, the ultimate question mark that has no answer to it.

My stealthy eye fixed on the naked bodies enveloped in steaming, torn curtains emergent from hot water, I watched Madame K.'s breasts touch the man's back while she rinsed him. I found nothing obscene or to be ashamed of in there. Instead, I was moved by their innocence, blameless, defenceless innocence. The unknown world condensed to a song between angels and men.

A sound startled me. I turned my eyes to chase the bright summer kimono gliding behind the chipped planks, her hair bobbing up and down, and her sash flying in the wind. There was a girl's head sticking up over the top of the curving fence into the tarn, and in her wake, a fountain of butterflies burst open like a snow-free snow day –

I forgot to mention. Apart from the gorgeous mountains, these hot springs were famous for the millions of butterflies and moths that came here to lay eggs. The hilly lands were shielded in an armour of most stunning colours, antique white eggshell, ghost blue, splashed hot pepper, minty peach honeydew, and misty black like dark lace on powdered skin...As I looked closer, I saw that some of the wings were damaged, perhaps in battles. Or did they fly too close to one another during the merrymaking flight? Suddenly, I understood what Madame K. was talking about during our lunchtime. My father undertook the annual trips to the South to collect butterflies! The walls of the inn were dressed with the work of my father as a self-declared naturalist. It was a shroud made of countless fragile bodies on pinheads. Death in frames. Sacrificed lives so their beauty can be admired. Until this day, the spectacle haunts me. My father and I didn't develop a warm relationship during his life, although I doubt if it has anything to do with the childhood trip for my part; maybe all parental love can be summed up as slavery to a pattern. As for my father, I'm not sure whether I lived up to the image of "real man" he had wanted his son to be.

Transfixed by the vision, I couldn't move my body in water – I didn't dare to – and my eyes riveted on the rosy, radiant face behind a cascade of hundreds of tangled, broken wings. Fragile, flawed, and wonderful, like life. Now the girl saw me at last. Turning a light shade of red she called out to her mother indignantly:

"Okaasan, why didn't you tell me...?!"

But she didn't turn away, and I looked into the almond-shaped slits of eyes framed with splendid lashes under two thick, dark arches of eyebrows, my breath caught in my chest. At this moment, I heard my father muttering the breathless words: "Musume-san, she is a true beauty!"

And so I made myself believe that the man came for the daughter, her mother was an excuse. Actually, my father used another word. He said: "Your daughter is a genuine *yamato nadeshiko*."

Yamato nadeshiko. I will reveal the significant meaning of these words in a while.

"You exaggerate, girl," her mother scolded her in a teasing manner. "He is only a child. And you, you are old enough to be his aunt. You will take care of him, won't you?"

Now it was Madame K. that exaggerated. Two months before I had proudly turned seven. Musume-san was aged round about seventeen. Besides, the word "aunt" reminds me of this big, broad-shouldered creature. Musume-san was airily frangible if not elusive, so delicate as if even touching her can cripple her for life.

Like so, I was left to the hands of my caregiver. She would come to fetch me every morning first thing. We would go for a walk in the hills together and stay long days away roaming up and down the mountain slopes, chasing after a special butterfly spotted by Musume-san. I suppose our parents found it convenient too for them to do whatever they did in our absence.

One day, after a failed quest for a golden swallowtail, we took a breather and sat down in the shades of pines. I told

Musume-san what I thought of my father. I said he was an evil and wicked man. I said it appalled me to think what he did to the pretty little creatures. Musume-san believed he did it for her mother because he *liked* her. I didn't have the courage to refute her, I didn't want to either. I let her talk.

"Your father hoards the ones that have just broken through the cocoon and shake their brand new wings in first light. He told me once that he is intrigued by emerging beauty and grace, the strength to regard change as joyful, not traumatic. I'm not sure I understood him. For us mountain dwellers, butterfly is a messenger. Our memories live forth through them. Fleeting, passing memories that would survive us. Butterflies have the power to defy time. Butterflies don't die, they transform. They spread a new pair of wings each time and take to the air. They are the immortal ones."

She struck a chord in my heart when I heard her saying the bittersweet words. I wanted to kiss her beautiful face in the thin light and tell her that I will love her forever. But words of a seven-year-old probably didn't count for her – if they didn't sound completely foolish.

"I don't think your father is an evil man," she said after a while. "These are smalls habits, well pursued betimes of man. But when evil is committed with a dignified cause, that is when we turn our world into hell."

Have the mountains taught the girl that wisdom?

Time passed quickly when we had these fleeting conversations, whose meaning eluded us at the time they were spoken. And suddenly, it was time for my father and me to go home.

It was one day before we took our planned leave. Musume-san came to find me when we were finishing some *onsen tamago* (eggs cooked in hot spring) and steamed rice for breakfast. She said she wanted to show me a secret spot we hadn't been before.

We walked for miles along the hilly brow, watching the village dwindle behind the grizzled mist like a forgotten song. In the belly of climbs soaring higher than turbid clouds, a dot of red temple tower levitating from leaden rock face.

"Look!"

I followed her pointing finger to patches of green and brown earth. On the potholed, eroded slope, a stretch of blossom field brandishing like fury. We were facing a track that led us into the flowering ocean of cool, bright, silky colours. The light turned murky at once, we could barely see our faces. From time to time the winding tendrils of twigs heavy from wine-coloured blooms would allow a thin blade of light to impale the semi-dark. No twitter of birds, something large was squawking from a nearby perch of silent, flowery promises that seemed to ooze a crimson liquid. Afterwards it became so quiet that I thought I heard her heartbeats like fallen leaves kissing the soil. I heard myself panting from excitement. But then, on a sultry breeze a blossom swung to my face, which I smelt: I smelt her trembling, tea-scented breath. Her hair, wet from sweat, tickled my cheeks. I felt her mouth on mine, an unlikely touch of syrupy, warm petals, and before I knew, it had floated past, leaving me in awe of life's delicate oddity.

With that kiss my childhood paradise ended.

During the night before our departure, a light rain fell, followed by a cloudy morning the next day. At noon, we were about to board the cart to the station. My father asked me to hurry or else we would miss our train. I insisted that we must wait for Musume-san who hadn't shown up since the evening before. Seeing his lack of efficiency, my father settled on a change of strategy, and threatened to leave without me, when I caught the rustling sound of silk kimono which made my heart tilt, the perplexing and unlikely feeling between pain and bliss.

On a shuffle of steps she came into view, tailing a golden fountain of swallowtails in her track. She halted across the blustery path, arrested in a sphere of rainbow obsidian wings flitting around her maidenly face. She cupped her hands, and closed them immediately to whisper something through her curled fingers. And then, the way she browsed her lips on mine, she kissed the frisky wings on her palm, sending it off a marvelled flight on her syrupy breath. This was my last picture of Musume-san.

Time passed, carrying me along its torrential streams. As I grew older, I made several attempts to write Musume-san a letter. I wanted to ask her what was the wish she had given her airborne messenger to be brought into the world. I never wrote that letter. In fact I wouldn't hear about both women until many years later. The devastating news was to alter the course of my life, for good or for evil. Destiny's music go on forever, destiny forever ever tracing Newton's ground.

My father never took me on another butterfly trip again. As far as I know he didn't return to the hills either after we had left. I didn't ask. I assumed Madame K. and her daughter had embarked the ship as planned and left for the Northeast of China. I tried to have a clear picture of their new life in Manchuria without knowing that soon I would be sent there myself, as a soldier.

But I couldn't forget Musume-san. In the evening, when alone in bed, I would remember the taste of her lips. Tormented by her absence, feeling blessed by it, I would take out the lucky stone she gave to me as keepsake when we stood under the flowers, daring not to breathe from yearnings that didn't have a name yet.

"It's a rain stone from the Yangtze river," she had told me. "Nanking stone is the symbol of hope. My mother and I are leaving Japan to find us a new home, we need to move on. One day I will visit Nanking to find a new stone in the Yangtze river. This one is for you."

The stone of hope.

I had never seen anything like it before, cinnabar sky, streaked with meteorite rain. Hope is not ordinary if it looks like this stone, I thought. Hope is not ordinary if it's out there in a river for us to pick it up and hold in hand. In the dark, I cried hot tears to make myself useful despite my useless self.

Years rolled away while I held out my hand to the bright vision. In the dead of night I would twitch open my eyes to find it erased from the shadowland of my room, before I saw it again in my mind's eye, unmistakable and even more vivid than the last that it almost hurt to look at: hope: the feathered creature perching on the canopied roof.

In the confused hours of losing faith and gaining it again, suddenly I became eleven. I grew to be this little person, rather conceited about my laughable amorous experience, with which I backed myself against my father. He never showed his disappointment in me explicitly, though. It was written on his face when he watched other boys of my age competing in samurai hardihood, as I fled to my room to read. I was not necessarily physically weak, as I recall now, but I didn't see much fun either in getting into terrible scraps with other men.

September 1931. I woke up one morning with a wet, sticky spot on my pyjama pants; it was not urine. Ashamed of myself and terribly frightened, I remembered my dream. I was walking in a deserted place where I came across an excited dog. I asked Musume-san to forgive me as I made a hustle to put on some fresh clothes, wrapping the dirty ones in an old bag I wanted to get rid of anyway. I hurried to the sitting room to find my father reading the morning paper.

"Great news!" he broadcasted once he saw me. "The Kwangtung Army took Manchuria! Aishingoro Puyi has sworn loyalty to our emperor!'

"Who is Aishingoro Puyi?" I asked, still feeling the swoons in my head.

"Puyi is the last Manchu emperor who reigned over China! Mark my words, son. Soon Japan will rule the entire region. I can hardly wait to see the day that the Empire of the Sun will encompass all of Asia!"

"I can't imagine why it's important to us," I snapped. I was annoyed maybe because for the first time I truly felt alone, a loneliness as if no-one, not a single person in the entire world ever knew me, not even myself.

My father looked alternately at my face and the newspaper on the table between us, his reading glasses flickering on the brim of his nose.

"Our emperor Hirohito is a wise man." He resolved to choose the effectively printed tall tale above any other options, the way he came to grips with reality. With a modest sigh he turns away from the hard-to-pin-down face that is life.

"Our emperor knows that in order to save our country and people, we must look outside and conquer other Asian races," he raised a voice as if to convince himself. "*Yamato Damashii* is superior. Japan should be the beacon of all weak races!"

Heart matters. Yamato Damashii, the Japanese heart.

I came across the idea for the first time in *Genji Monogatari*, a classic novel from the 11th century written by a certain court lady, Lady Shikibu. Nowadays literary critics split hairs as to whether Genji is the first novel ever written about human passion. The language especially was a trial for me at my young age. Loads of word puzzles and exemplary associations which are strange to the contemporary mind. However, I managed to unravel some of the storylines. One of them told about Prince Genji who was violently in love with Lady Fujitsubo. He couldn't fulfil his love because she was his stepmother. The prince then went to the mountains to find a girl who looked exactly like Lady Fujitsubo. He kidnapped the girl and brought her back to the palace where he raised her to become his lover.

Yamato Damashii came straight from a love story. And yet, over the centuries the original suggestion of a native virtue had been transformed so that in the end nothing in no respect, to no degree was left of Lady Shikibu's invention. Yamato Damashii was conveniently converted to the artless spirit of self-pride and military heroism. Offer your life at the feet of death. On top of that, the glory of Bushido was boosted up by the immense, religious respect for the Emperor.

Some additional information should be provided on the above. At the turn of the 20th century, the Japanese petty bourgeoisie class and working classes had found themselves increasingly able to participate in national policy debate, heralding a spanking era called the Taisho Democracy. A parliamentary government set foot in our native turf, with the promising image of a newborn Japan being transformed to a country of full-fledged democracy. We boasted to be the first forward-looking nation in the ancient, lethargic Asia. However, the end of 1920's already showed failures in providing an effective cure to the old wounds left of the deep-rooted, feudal past. With the death of the Taisho emperor in 1926, the forsaken transformation danced smoothly towards a new-old abyss. The era of Taisho democracy ended. The Showa era began, steeped in scented visions of unlimited growth and expansion. The militarism-driven emperor Tenno Hirohito proved to be a man of his time. Soon he would interfere with state matters and give his direct order to develop chemical weapons to subjugate China.

I glanced over the newspaper spread open in front of us. The black-and-white photo showed armed men arriving by train, marching into the Chinese city Mukuden in intimidating arrays, hailed by a throng of locals. I caught myself searching for the face I tried not to forget in my prayers.

"Otoosan?"

"Yes, Maru-chan?" I hated my father addressing me this way, I felt insulted by the diminutive. Above all, whatever he said seemed crookedly malicious that morning.

"You remember our trip to Madame K. and her daughter?" I asked, trying to sound natural enough.

"Sure I remember Musume-san. Why?"

"Back then you said something about her – "

"I said she was a real beauty, a genuine *yamato nadeshiko*."

"What does it mean? I know the flower. Fringed pink, isn't it?"

Ever since I was a child I knew to treat myself to the wild carnation coming into bud in the spring. The purplish pink shade announcing new start, throwing a rug of graceful and patient brocade over the hills like multipart painted screens. The gossamer scent made me feel giddy as a sparkling drop of dew.

"Amazing you don't know, Maru-chan, since you have your head in books all this time!" Surprised, my father arched an incredulous brow. "Yamato nadeshiko is a metaphor for the ideal of Japanese female beauty. She is the manifestation of Yamato damashii, the spirit of our Japanese race."

He paused to think about something.

"Madame K. wrote me a letter from Manchuria. It seems that Musume-san has responded to the call of our emperor. She became…She was…" My father was probably searching for an Homeric epithet, but I have no need for more words and reasoning of men. Musume-san, either forced by circumstances or driven by half-truths, had signed up for the "joy division" to serve the Imperial Army. She became a comfort girl for our soldiers.

I stared into my father's face, my chest heaving with shocks of anger.

"Things didn't go as they had expected," avoiding my eyes, my father continued in a sorry voice. "Musume-san sacrificed herself for our country and nation. She is a very brave girl, indeed. I think we should be very proud of our own Yamatoo Nadeshiko. Don't you agree, Maru-chan?"

Suddenly, I remembered the words she said to me. *When evil is committed with a dignified cause.*

Without saying a word, I stood up and ran to the door, I didn't want my father to see me in tears. I locked myself in my room for the rest of the day, feeling ashamed of whom we are, of our polished two faces. I cried for Musume-san. I cried for myself. Sobbing in silence, I decided that I will go to Manchuria to find Musume-san and bring her back home. There is only one way for me to do that. On that day I made the first choice in life. Ever since then I had been counting the days and months until I could finally sign up for the Imperial Army.

1936. I was sixteen. Japan took part in both the Winter and Summer Olympics, both hosted by Hitler's Germany.

On the 26th of February, I was in Tokyo to speak to a friend of my father's who offered to help me with choosing a major. I had cancelled my visit to the capital several times, since I was determined to join the Army as soon as the opportunity presents itself. I told nobody about my plan. Nobody, not even my father, knew that all the years I was waiting for the call of duty. I didn't care. After all, I was prepared to die in China.

It seemed a normal day in the capital, filled with the boring drudgery of everyday life. The gift of a perfectly ordinary day didn't come until in the evening. I went out to buy some food for dinner to find no soul on the streets but lots was happening behind the curtains. The attempted coup was all over in the newspaper.

The story goes that after the rebelling troops stormed the government headquarters, several of our country's leaders got killed. Armed men seized control of our capital. For a few days Tokyo was a nightmare. People were scared, nobody seemed to know what was going to happen next. Three days went by in tension so thick and sharp it would cut a knife. Then news reached us that the low-ranking military officers, the plotters of the government overthrow, were arrested. Our Emperor as the symbol of power and unity of the people passed his judgment and restored peace to the country. Japan escaped interior chaos only by a whisker.

However, the imperial verdict was followed by a purge led by high-ranking army officers. The right-wing nationalists saw the chance to expand their influence. They took over the control of power machine. Our country rushed towards war with China and the rest of the world. Every man, woman and child of Japan suddenly found themselves dancing on a tightrope.

Six months later, I received the imperial notice to join the Army. I packed immediately and returned to Tokyo. After stark, hard-nosed training, I was selected for a unit with a special mission. I knew this would be my last autumn I spent on my native soil; autumn is my favourite season when every leaf turns into a flower, and every face becomes a mosaic of memories. In the spring of 1937, for the first time in my life, I set foot on the land of my country's enemy. Previously, with help from friends, I had sought information as to the whereabouts of Madame K. and her daughter.

On a snowy winter evening in the same year, I went to see Madame K. at the teahouse she ran near the train station.

"*Ureshii wa.* Good evening, Maru-chan! You've grown into such a handsome young man! You were an adorable child. *Arigato ne.* Thanks for getting in touch."

Brushing snow from my uniform shoulders, Madame K. ushered me inside her cosy venue.

She was still the well-groomed woman I knew from my childhood, clean, neat nails, her head elegantly, humbly bowed. As she straightened to smile at me, she gave me a chill. Her face looked much older than her real age, her cheeks in a pale glow and completely drained, her tired, sunken eyes buried in the shadows of dull hoary hair which was once lustrous, jet-black charm.

I threw a quick glance about the place to find Musume-san not in attendance. It was quiet, the evening was still young. I assumed that the girl needs some sleep before she will receive her clients into the small hours. I was too embarrassed to ask.

I put my rifle on the table and took a seat. We didn't know what to say to each other with all the years between us. Time kills fantasy, that's why we have memory. We both kept silent.

"Tell me how you found me, Maru-chan. *And Why?*" Pouring me a cup of tea, Madame K. broke the ice.

"I'm home-sick. Aren't you, obasan?" I called her aunt like I did as a child. "I brought you this. It's almost New Year."

I took the rice cake out of my pocket to put it in front of her.

"You saved *o-mochi* from your rations for me?!"

With both hands she held up the little bundle. Peeling open the wrapping with meticulous fingers, she took a deep smell like a mother worshipping her newborn. Large tear drops threaded down the crisscross of her face.

"I knew a place in Tokyo where they sold the best o-mochi in the world. When I was a young girl, I always went there to buy the rice cakes for our New Year's celebration. Do you think we will see our home ever again, Maru-chan?"

Now it was my turn to feel like crying. I washed the lump in my throat down with a mouthful of tea.

"You want to know how I found you, obasan? I can tell you a terrific, sad story. If you want a happy ending, just tell me, and I can change it into a bad story, " I said, making a poor effort to fend off our melancholy.

"I want a perfect ending. Or a sad ending, albeit a happy one. How a story ends gives meaning to how it began. *Sumimasen.* Tell me when did you arrive in China? Did you ask for permission to leave the camp? Do they treat you well? You can't be an officer at your age…You are now…?"

"I will be eighteen in a couple of months. I'm with a special unit, intelligence is our task."

"That sounds logical. Back then you told me you wanted to become a writer. Are writers intelligent people?"

"I should think it's extremely improbable to call anyone who plods along with books intelligent these days. So I guess I changed my mind. I draw lines."

I added quickly at her inquisitive expression, "We gather information of a new place before our large troop arrives. We make maps. It has been some time now since I got my first job."

Madame K. looked at me briefly, touching her gingerly fingers to the rifle.

"Do you have to kill people to do what you do?"

"I'm trained to hide. If that's not good enough, yes, I pull the trigger and shoot."

I didn't say anything about my secret most probably out of male pride. During my military training I had made myself famous by collapsing a number of times upon hearing gunfire. I fainted at the sound of bullets – which I suppose was the reason for me to be selected as an intelligence worker whose talent for hiding is favoured above shooting skills. The latter may lead to giving away your unit's position. I was a skilled sniper though, my father would have been proud of me. He was one of our many countrymen who believed "a Rich Country has a Strong Military". Besides, it seems that through reading many books, I indeed became more experienced, more clever and intelligent over the years. That is to say, I anticipate new situations and keep my wits about me in dangers and crisis. They didn't have the wrong guy when they picked me out of hundreds of young soldiers to do what I do.

"Where are you heading to next?" she asked again.

"We don't know yet. We don't have any information until we have to. The four of us leave at once for our assigned mission. Cesaru is our superior, we follow his orders, only he carries a revolver. The other three soldiers, me, Suzuki-san and Sato-san, we are each given a rifle to defend ourselves."

"*Soo ne.* I understand," she nodded, pouring me more tea from which I took a sip. It tasted divine and made me remember good things in life that I had forgotten. I drained the cup, and wiped my mouth on the back of my hand.

"Yesterday I eavesdropped Cesaru-san on the field phone. I heard our commander repeating the name of a place."

I reached into my breast pocket and dug out the rain stone lying round and crimson in my palm.

"Musume-san gave me this when we visited you years ago. Back then she told me that she wanted to go to Nanking to find another stone in the Yangtze river. It seems I will be in Nanking sooner than she. She called it the stone of hope… "

Suddenly I stopped talking. Mortified and disturbed, I watched her entire body crease as if she was dying from such pain and agony that she even lacked the desire to cry.

"Musume-san is no longer with us," she murmured the weak words in the end, struggling to lift her head to look at me, her face ghoulishly waxen, her lips crusted and white, her entire body shaking, shivering to bits. "My daughter died last year."

"*Dead?* How?" I swallowed hard.

She grabbed the tea I poured for her and downed it in one. Slowly, she regained her strength.

"Are you sure you want to hear this?" Her shoulders slumped, she asked in her broken voice.

"I don't but tell me," I insisted.

She heaved a deep sigh, uncertain for a moment.

"Well, your father must have told you. After you left, we sold our business and packed for Manchuria. Musume-san and I had had some arguments. The future lies ahead of us, even though the future is not the same as it was before, we were both in for a change. It's my fault, I made her believe Manchuria is the future!

"There were a lot of talk about the north-eastern region with its rich resources. Our Emperor made plans to turn Manchukuo into a powerhouse. We were pioneers when we arrived here. Business was not lucrative in the beginning, but we managed. And then, when our Army came in 1931, things changed overnight. Certainly, Manchukuo was part of our Empire and the soldiers made our teahouse flourish. However, the militaries intimidated and terrorised the local Chinese, arbitrary arrests and extortion were a widespread practice. We became what we hate to be.

"Musume-san volunteered to offer her service to our clients. She believed it's the least she could do to help our country win the war. We heard stories about women of Japan who sacrifice themselves for the glorious future of our people. I think she felt guilty. I didn't try to talk her out of it. What else is there for us to do, us women on that road! Everything seemed to go well at first. My daughter was popular with men. You remember what your father said about her?"

"*Yamato nadeshiko*. My father saw in her the ideal of Japanese female beauty – "

"One year ago, a man came in dressed as a high-ranking officer. The money was good. The next morning when she didn't come for tea, I went upstairs to look for my daughter. The room was empty; my daughter was gone. Two days later the police found her body near the city wall. The man took her so many times that her underside was bruised and in tatters. Then he took his knife to cut off her breasts and left her to die. It was…" Unable to complete her sentence, she covered her mouth with her hands to hold back her tears and sick.

She carried on with her story. I couldn't hear a thing she was saying to me, only her mouth moved. My mind went blank. I felt as if punched in my face. Hot stings pulsating in my head, acid stars burning on my cheeks. I felt my inside gutted out with a cold axe. Never before did I realise how much I loved the girl. I didn't know I'm capable of such anger, the venom soaked my every bone and ate into my last nerves.

Suddenly, I heard myself interrupting the remote drone of her voice:

"Who is the swine? Did the police find any trace who did it?" I hissed, surprised how cool I sounded, I was on the brink to kill myself for not keeping an eye on her.

"They said he was a communist. But you never know…it could be propaganda again. We receive leaflets every day to tell us how brave our Imperial Army is fighting the evil called Communism. A perverse ideology, if you ask me, trying to take the world by prophecies and palmistry. I'm not sure lying is better. We have built our Empire on lies. That's all I have to say. Now go, soldier," she stood up abruptly. "I'm tired. I'm ashamed of myself. I don't want to see you again. And you keep this one. I think Musume-san is happy to know that Maru-chan has her heart." She put the blood-red stone in my palm and closed my fingers.

I looked at her shattered eyes for the last time. We will never see each other again. Hearing Musume-san's story, knowing it, changed me, irrevocably, as a human being.

A storm raged inside me as I took to dark night, lurching along forlorn rail tracks in the icy moonshine, calculating my steps and counting dirty, black chimneys in the feather-white winter to keep myself together. If before today I felt confused about anything at all, now my country's enemy had a clear image in front of my eyes. He is not longer an idea out of the poet's abstract head, but touchable and real as my knees and thighs:

He is my enemy.

A few months went past since my visit to Madame K.'s teahouse. Finally one day, we received orders to leave at once. We were sent on a secret operation in the South. 300 kilometre west-northwest of Shanghai, outside the city wall of Nanking, to be exact.

The scenery of the Yangtze delta took our breath away. We couldn't believe that we were taking a holiday break in the thick of war. When asked why we deserve this and what were our assigned tasks, our commander Cecaru was reluctant to elaborate, saying only, "Wait and see, soldiers. This time I can give you real war." Cesaru came to China to become a real soldier killing real people, not some women's stuff like drawing landscapes.

"*Wakarimashita!* Yes, Commander! We hate the Communist bandits as much as you do. One problem. They are damn good guerrilla fighters. I can be one if I had hills pretty as these." Sato-san speculated. Turning to me, he poked me in the ribs.

"Mate," he spoke in a low, joking voice. "Guard your ear plugs with your life. They will steal your honour."

Sato-san and I knew each other from the Intelligence School where we were taught two things: hiding and how to conduct guerrilla warfare. He knew the chink in my armour. During a training session, he thought I shot myself, and when he found out that I merely lost consciousness after hearing gunshots, he helped me to make up a story.

He was the heir of the Tajima trading company in Osaka. Being the oldest son of his parents, he was expected to take over the family business in a few years – if there was still something left of it, he said. On the day when Sato-san was summoned to join the Army and serve our Emperor and country, he was celebrating his twentieth birthday.

Sato-san made me realise that we were anything but supermen, and it was nothing to be ashamed of. At the military school he was already notoriously hypochondriac. Now he carried oily green little cakes around to rub on his skin and keep mosquitoes at a distance. I thought I would die from the inflamed lumps all over my body. He used to wear white gloves. He even refused to take them off in bed, to the great irritation of our commander, who still held him responsible for a blind attack by our invisible enemy in the dead of night. I knew he also stored a quantity of stolen eau de cologne – with which I would kill lonely, dark hours in my quest for an anonymous woman, drinking from the little bottles to keep myself warm. But by then, wild flowers would have covered Sato-san's grave along an unfamiliar road.

Outside the city wall of Nanking, we moved daily from one position to the next along the riverbank, reporting through telegrams and receiving new orders. We remembered to hold our fire when the enemy was not firing and kept safe shelter in the woods. We remembered to dig deep, stand-up foxholes, which are better than slit trenches and give you protection except under direct artillery attack. We drew up plans for more holes we covered with leaves and flowering trunks – the spring smelt like a shy maiden – and we could hardly wait for the day when we would crawl in and resist until some explosive or a human terrier kill us. We remembered all the lessons we had learned at the School. None of these was actually put into practice. It seemed strangely peaceful during the entire course of our mission as we lurked under the old city wall, waiting for the BIG thing to happen. The change of season caught four men huddling together in the rain. As soon as the rain stopped, we searched for food. Sometimes we attacked a villager to steal his chicken. We fired on people we ran into along the way, because we were made to believe that everybody who dresses himself like a Chinese is either a spy or a member of the resistance forces. We were a bundle of nerves, hungry and scared. Once we shot a group of students. Two boys were killed at once. A girl survived our fire. She told us that they were passing the river on their 1,000 mile journey to Kunming; the city in the remote part of the country operated as makeshift quarters for the universities disbanded due to war. Which we knew was the truth. But when Cesaru found a suspicious-looking calligraphy scroll in her luggage, our commander was convinced that she was a communist spy. "Where do you hide this lot of brainwash rubbish? Show me quickly!" he yelled at her. Without waiting for answer, he pulled the trigger on his revolver, blasting a hole in her face. Her head exploded like a giant mushroom, pink and white churning out. The quiet, gluey sound still makes me shiver at night. The months living outside the city gate built a prison of distrust around us. Isolated from the rest of the world, every person appeared to be our enemy.

And then, an early summer kicked in with skies of blue and clouds of white. The bright blessed day when we were yet to know ourselves better. This is the day we have been waiting for only to find out that we are animals arrayed in human skin.

At the end of 1937, the Japanese Imperial Army captured Shanghai after a hard-fought battle. Many of us lost our friends and brothers. With help from our navy, Shanghai fell.

Tokyo decided to expand the war to Nanking, the then Chinese capital. By now the Chinese authorities already knew that the fall of Nanking was simply a matter of time. Accordingly, the governmental seat was moved to Chongking, a mountainous city a thousand miles away. An agreement had been reached between the two countries, but the deal collapsed in the last-minute negotiation. The Chinese side made the final decision to withdraw armed forces and preserve the soldiers for future battles. Chinese troops retreated and ran away like rats. Nanking was left undefended.

However, the people of Nanking were ordered to stay. Citizens must fight to the death and they must by no means surrender. To prevent civilians from fleeing the city, small military units were installed to guard the port. Roads were blocked, boats were destroyed and burnt in the harbour. To further discourage evacuation, private homes, buildings, scrub woods, and sometimes an entire village were set ablaze to become a burning firewall around the city. By the time the front position of the Japanese army was in sight, advancing, pouring over the long, curving shore of the Yangtze river like an ink-coloured tsunami, the tacit consent had been reached among the officers and men that they could loot and rape as they wish.

The four of us finally came out of our dark recesses to join our troop marching into battle with an unprotected, unarmed, chanceless opponent exposed to rampant atrocity and endemic carnage. When I read Milton, I used to wonder how demons could build Pandemonium, the capital of Hell in about an hour. Now I know you can. Nanking was hell on earth that day, handed over to demons in human shape, demons with an empty heart, with a heart made of stone.

Demons at large, running in all directions for women and warm food, shouting in a language I understood.

Cesaru, our commander ordered us to stay together. At one point, a brigade paraded past us. Our commander recognised the officer from his hometown.

"We received orders to encourage the national fighting spirit. Do you like sport?" the officer yelled at us in a throwaway manner.

"Sure we do. *Is she good?*" our commander answered, bursting into coarse laughter. He motioned for us to follow.

We walked through shattered piles of debris and smoking houses torn from smoking houses, drawn to the noises. In spite of the mayhem happening under our nose, the summer air had a curious tranquillity indelibly printed in my memories. I will never forget the faces gazing at me from the naked depths of our shame and committed crime –

In a big, burnt void, Chinese civilians were lined up in two rows. Hundreds of men, women and children, silent as the grave. Nobody made a sound because there is NO human sound that could be uttered that could indicate or describe the horror.

Two soldiers were called forward. Two boys, barely men, each holding a sword in their hands. Fine katana blades, sharp and erect, displayed in superior swordsmanship style, with the right hand touching the hilt guard and the left clenched at the chilly metal end. The brilliant steel gleaming with blue greyish lustre, the sharpness curving into strength. We love the pretty sight of it, wonderfully picturesque, wonderfully cruel and cruelly wonderful. The scenic splendour stirs our blood, ignites our soul, rouses our slow body to action. Holding a killing weapon makes us feel full and great, our fabrication of glamour moves us to tears. We are a nation that has a penchant for theatre!

On the officer's signal, two soldiers started racing along massive walls made of living people. Both of them had decided on his favourite part to run his katana blade skewed at a tasteful, flawless angle, and catching sudden glints of metal that blinds the magpie eyes. Heads, taking flight on wings of bouncy hair. A girl's satin ribbon unfurling, a wind-blown, silent blossom, suspended in spots of liquid scarlet, and her shining eyes as good as dead, not dead enough to close themselves. The sound caught me by surprise. A formation of large and small hailstones hit the ground, mixed with dirty blood. The sound of rounded weights chilled me to the marrow. Black, big marbles thundered in a dark menacing cloud of stirred dust, rolling together to find their peace of mind in the pit only a few yards away from my feet. In the suffocating silence somebody clapped his hands. An ovation of a different kind followed. I cheered and applauded along, as more volunteers unsheathed their deadly ornament; they can't wait to test the quality of their treasured heirloom. These are my people vying to cut the most heads with one single blow of sword! Their merriment made my head swim, the sort high spirits we knew ever since we were children taking part in the annual Bushido tournaments. *Gyokusai* we were taught. Glorious death. Gloriously killing. It's our ancient culture we have inherited from our ancient ancestors. We were proud of our ancientness that we showed without care in the world like child's play, bad eggs, chain tag, capture the flag. There is always a winner and a loser. A man finds his identity by identifying. Suddenly I caught myself in an extremely elated state of euphoria. Why ruin our little party in hard times? Let's *kanpai!* Cheers to insanity, our code of honour! It was pretty powerful. But if I say so, I'm lying. We were heroes who feared to run away. Your fear to be rejected by your countrymen is so much stronger. Fear is the mother of all wars, not courage, not bravery.

I turned away to shut myself, I felt sick, on the verge of frenzy. I looked for my unit members in the crowd when I heard our commander's voice. Cesaru was talking to the officer from his hometown.

"How long does this take, Captain Atsushi? We are thirsty – stayed in the damn bushes too long and fed the damn mosquitoes – we go find a coffeehouse in the neighbourhood – tell your soldiers to join us – "

We followed our commander to an elegant street, the last one in shape.

"*Sugoi!* This looks more like it!" Suzuki-san banged open the door with his rifle.

The café was dark inside, curtains were drawn. It took us a while longer to see things, and when we did, we were surprised to find a girl standing behind the bar. She didn't run. She didn't move a hair as if paralysed. Four men, we were speechless, intimidated by her calmness. Four men, we lowered our guns as one, her strength was invincible and stubborn. Her face showed no emotion, only her eyes burned, and through her eyes we saw ourselves. For the first time, we realised what we were. We felt ashamed. We were foul, panic-stricken beasts doing what we did without knowing what we did, without knowing *why*.

Suzuki-san took a step forward to point his bayonet at her. Our commander curbed him. He turned to smile at the girl, considering her for a few seconds, studying her face, her eyes, everything.

"We are thirsty, miss," he said, putting a light tone in his oily voice, his hand making a drinking gesture. We followed our commander to the jacquard silk settee.

The girl walked to the window and drew open the curtains. She had on a jade-green summer dress with soft bamboo prints, the kind of body-hugging one-piece garment worn by urban Chinese women. She was fine and petit, her young body already showing the magical curves through the gauzy fabric. I assumed she was the daughter of the owner. But why didn't she hide herself? She must be completely out of her mind to have stayed here, with curtains drawn, dressed like that! Our eyes glued to her body in her narrow dress, chased after her tiny paces to the bar. She poured four glasses with the clear liquid from a bottle and carried the tray to our table. Whirling around to leave, she said something I didn't understand. Our commander seized her by her wrist, his other hand reaching for the cold drink.

"*Thank you, China*," he whispered, his mouth almost touching her face. She turned a little pale. His words startled her. She didn't expect any of us would actually speak her mother tongue. Cesaru was the only one who had had a proper language training at the Intelligence School. "Fair is foul and foul is fair. May Imperial heavens blind me if I tell a lie. Pigs sound better!" Our commander once gave his tongue-lashing judgement.

He put the glass to his lips and took an endless swig, throwing back his head. He raised his emptied glass, his throat pulsing, his pink tongue painting the corner of his mouth. A grin surfaced on his face sharp as a razor.

"I say, are you all alone by yourself, *Wong Down Lo*?" he pronounced in a husky sound.

We laughed nervously, watching the girl who ever sought to break loose of his grip lumpy and yellow with calluses.

"Suzuki-san!" our commander barked, signalling the solider to jam her way out between table and chairs.

Cesaru stared at her offensively, speaking in a low, vulgar voice, making a dimple in the blue silk settee with his finger.

"You me happy, Miss Chinatown?" The grin on his face jerked, his smile disappeared.

"Tell me about yourself, you shameless whore. Don't lie to the Imperial Army officer, we are very friendly people. Don't make me angry with you. I know why you stayed behind, speak the truth. What is your business here besides Blow Yu, huh? Some things I can't change. I have this funny smell. This is the place where the red cockroaches meet, isn't it? These communists THINK like filthy cockroaches! Suzuki-san, search her! Make sure she doesn't hide the hot cockroach shit anywhere."

Dutifully, the soldier shoved his bayonet under her dress, giving us a flash of her cotton knickers. Our commander's eyes rolled. Inch by inch, he rose from his place, crouching down his face over hers, forcing her to back out. She toppled over, her head hit on something hard. She cried out, rolling down to the bench with the rifle between her leg. A drop of blood trickled unhurriedly down a horizontal cut in her torn stockings onto the sky blue silk. We didn't know where to look, but we couldn't resist to look at her. Three layers of fear and vulnerability make the woman. That's the awful truth of men, the awful revolutionary history of women. We were so strained and excited we could have shit our pants.

"Everybody gets his turn, soldiers!" Our commander shouted orders, removing his revolver from its holster to put it away on the tray, unbuttoning, lowering himself. He pressed his entire body on her to pin her down, wrapping her tussling arms, leaving her windmilling legs to thrash about every which way they could. She looked like a capsized insect.

We were too tense and too occupied with our sickening game to notice the hand reaching out a cluster of chairs. Suddenly, the boy stood in front of us, facing us with courage. In his hand he held our commander's revolver.

"LET HER GO," he hissed through his teeth, putting the gun on Cesaru's nape, his finger ready to squeeze the trigger. Cesaru straightened to pull his pants up, showing his uncovered rear-end in full light. He looked disgusting. We waited in silence, one that could drive someone mad, when Sato-san suddenly let go a squeaking cry as if he realised how upset he was. Then came the sound of gunfire. Next Sato-san slumped in his chair, bending forward, sitting up straight in stiffened spasms. I squirted forward to catch my friend in my arms. I didn't faint; I didn't know I didn't. Blood gushed out of the bullet hole in his leg which I tried to stop with the towel I took from my waist to bind his wound.

"You are fine, Sato-san," I put him down in the puddle of blood. "I'm going to take care of this. Then we drink our drink and walk out of here and go home. I'm taking you home. You hear me? *Osakajo*. You still have to show me the castle in your hometown. You can't die. Promise me you don't die. Not now, not yet. Please, my friend…"

I rattled on, seeking comfort in words, wiping my soaked hands on my soldier's uniform. I was horrified to see so much blood pouring out of him. The tepid smell of rust made my stomach turn, sending shivers through my body up to my head. I was so frightened, I broke out in a cold sweat. In the corner of my eyes, I witnessed the unspeakable tableaux, lucid as gravity, a silent movie playing in ultra-slow motion:

The boy takes aim at us again. Kicked from behind, losing his footing, he slides away to fall prey to strong, hostile arms. His gun flying through the air like a clumsy, black bird. Another shot goes off, and for a moment, the girl's stifled screaming stops so that we can hear her quiet, trembling breath, as if anticipating disaster with every question or putting fear of gods into the moment that the bayonet's bright light sinks into her flesh. The icy, sharp edge cutting her jade-green summer dress in one long-lasting move, revealing her soft belly in harsh daylight. Her blood falling all over what remained of her clothes to conceal her state of undress. It hurts so much. She wants the pain to stop, even if stopping the pain means stopping everything, forever. She wants her torture to end.

"Take me, pig!" she utters the words sparse and sinewy like a silky thread. "Rape me, dirty pig! I beg you to rape me!"

Unable to move, the boy reaches out to her. He knowingly turns his face away. He is forced to turn back to see her, her useless tussle under the abysmal bulk of human shame. He feels confused. On her face is a hidden map of a hidden world. It's a mixed expression of pleasure and disgust. She is the girl who made him stop being a kid. *In her frightened eyes he caught a shadow of thrilled spark...*

Shocked at his own thoughts, regardless of his guilty self-chastisement, he is uncertain if it's right for him to think in these words not easily described in words. If thinking would undo her pain, he'll do it even when words are lies. If truth would stop this all at once! If lies would make women in China less ashamed of themselves!

His bewilderment pales his young face. He wants to scream and attack the man, yet he holds his rage in check. To do otherwise would mean the end of her life. Powerlessly, he watches her blood paint the jacquard silk warps crimson…

My vision blackened. A great numb feeling washed over me as I let go of all, the past and the future. I was out cold, frozen by hysterics, fear, and self-loathing. Then, from an unreal distance, I heard them coming. With a rending roar the door of the café was crashed open. A swarm of foulest creatures surging forward, with the officer in the front, bustling past me, followed by vermin cries in his wake. Well-bred men showing their true skin, yelping and bellowing, crude language, feet all over the place. The war zoo is loose. Dinner is ready.

"Get me out of here," I caught my friend's weak voice in the havoc.

Shoring him up across my shoulders, I pushed my way through more soldiers pouring into the tight doorway.

In the middle of the livid-coloured palette of the doomed Earth, I found a little brook to lay down my friend. I felt a funeral in my head, so cheerless so inconsolable. I am the one who is buried alive on this day. We didn't dare to speak. We didn't dare to look. We HAVE to look. In front of our eyes a wide panorama showing a complete lawlessness, there is no rule at all, a situation when anything can happen and *happened*. We were caught forever in a trap we can't walk out. We were caught in an inescapable network of terror and cold-blooded violence with utter disregard for life, so excessively and extravagantly pitiless and brutal that hearing Apocalypse would be like hearing an aesthete's joke. Streets were littered with bullet casings, and black smoke billowed from homes and buildings set ablaze by soldiers for a laugh. Ancient wooden doors lying busted, and burning on stoves scattered on street corners. Cradles overturned, baby clothes in the trees.

Citizens of Nanking fleeing in all directions only to be taken down like rabbits. Dead bodies of abused women and young girls left uncovered. Living bodies breaking out the towers of human flesh, crawling naked on all fours, searching for hope at the end of the day and hoping to be another day older underneath the velvet heaven where every dream is broken…

I wanted to wash myself just to do something to keep me from seeing even if for a second. I put my hand out to feel around the fast running water. Something was wrong, I didn't understand. And I shrieked. Until today I'm not sure whether it was my distraught imagination. As I cupped my hands in the brook, it felt warm and sticky. It was a fast running river of blood, never ending, surrounded by silent darkness.

Silence is more than words! Silence bore more evidence than words on that day!

Resting in my arms, Sato-san was going out like the snuff of a candle. I need to look for help. I can't feel my legs. I didn't want to feel them, I wanted to be done. At sunset I saw two men among tracks of ruins and cinders, approaching us at a jog trot. Suzuki-san saw us first and waved his rifle at us. I heard our commander talking in a loud voice. I didn't understand what was going on really. Everything revolved around me like a surreal soup, with warped loops of a mouth going speeding round a million bends of my brain. Everything around me refused to become reality. Suddenly I felt the punch on my chest, and found myself hurrying back to Monday. I heard my orders:

"*Bakayaro!* Don't stare at me like an idiot! I said: Find my revolver and bring it back to me immediately! Go! We will take Sato-san to the infirmary."

I moved, and followed my legs to the café to find a soldier busy dipping carpet and curtains in gasoline, pouring more on woodwork, his other hand waving a torch.

"Are you nuts?" he shouted at me. But my legs won't stop. They took me into the sea of flames. Red streaked white tongues of fire licking my face and feet, unfathomable tongues, cleansing tongues, sad, healing tongues that reveal the right words…When I emerged again into the sunlight from the looming black smoke like a miracle, I was a newborn man, purged with blood and defects, purged of his violence. I blew up the roads and burned down my bridges.

I made the second choice in life. I reached a crucial decision, an imperative which I can't ignore and which I must obey without delay.

"So what exactly did you decide?"

It was two years later that Sato-san put the question to me. The two of us had been hiding for two bloody years, moving about in the marshes along the river, living off small, skimpy meals. We couldn't turn back to our unit, because Cesaru had probably reported us as "leak", and we imagined all kinds of humiliations for discredited and dishonoured deserters. Once Sato-san, in his good-will, heroic mood, even suggested that we turn over to our enemy, though neither one of us considered it a real option. *What if they treated us like we did them, in Nanking?* The thought of that day made us tremble like cold babies. Every so often Sato-san would wake me screaming in the dark, and I had to find something to clog his feverish exclamation marks so we would not be heard. The wound on his leg was getting worse again. I tried all kinds of herbs, but I couldn't save him, not this time. One of these days my only friend will die.

"What happened after you went back into the burnt coffeehouse? Did you find Cesaru's revolver?" Sato-san attempted the same question in a different way.

"Why don't you ask me what I saw in the shambles?"

"She was such a beauty, wasn't she? I will never forget the girl in her jade-green summer dress, pouring us a drink behind the bar. She looked like a Madonna."

"She looked like a painting, so unreal."

"You saw her again, didn't you? Tell me about her. I want to die thinking of something nice and kind..."

A little star flickered in Sato-san's fading eyes. Suddenly it was more than I could take. I burst into tears, my entire body shaking like mad.

"Yes, I saw her, Sato-san," I held my friend's hand in mine, persuading him to stay alive and stay with me.

"Did you smile to her when you saw her? My mom said a smile is a curve that sets everything straight. *Did you?*" he urged in a weak voice.

"I did, Sato-san," I lied.

The true sequences are thus. I ran into the fire. I found the revolver immediately because it was the only thing that was not burning. Everything was illuminated around me, the environs, my thoughts. The strong smell of gasoline ignited something in me. Suddenly I knew I wouldn't be returning to my unit. I got away from the suffocating fumes, I didn't know how but I did. Then I waited until the next morning to look for Sato-san at the improvised sickbay nearby. He was in a corner to himself. They had removed the bullet but he couldn't sleep from pain. There was no medicine, my friend said when he saw me. Buddy, I came to say good-bye, I said. Take me with you, he said. Are you sure? Please, you are my only friend! So I put Sato-san in a spare set of clothes I found in a house. Together we stole out of the infirmary at the crack of dawn, leaving behind us our guns and soldier's uniform. We had declared war against our country. Now we were on our own.

At first Sato-san did pretty well. We managed without medicine and bandages, and his wound healed. Then winter came, his health started to deteriorate, quicker than I had expected. When the warm weather came at last, his calf had turned slowly into a crawling anthill filled with pus and a white army of maggots. He couldn't even lie down properly. There was nothing I could do to help my friend.

"Yes, I saw her, Sato-san," I held his hand growing colder and heavy in mine. "And I smiled at her, you know why? Because that's the language we both spoke. She was lying on the blue silk bench, with her eyes closed, as if she was asleep. Somebody dressed her back in her jade-green summer clothes."

"Yeah, it looked good on her. I'd like to remember her that way, her skin as white as snow, her lips as red as blood, her hair as black as ebony..." My friend indulged in the fairytale. He remembered the exact words by Andersen he liked to be read to. He had an incredible memory for details and dates, I could only begin to imagine how insufferable this war must be for someone like him.

"*Was she dead?*" he asked suddenly. "I wish she was dead. I can't bear to think her living on with all that had happened to her. Tell me she was dead."

"Yes, she was dead, Sato-san," I mumbled, sobbing. She was.

"And the boy who shot me?"

"He was dead too," I lied once more.

"They rested next to each other, like two angels sharing a sweet dream," I kept up with my untruth, my hand held tightly onto the weighing cold. Sato-san made the last effort to squeeze in my palm. I reached out to check his breath, and closed his eyes. All the while I didn't stop talking, I wanted to finish my story. This time the truth.

"They rested next to each other, like two angels sharing a sweet dream. The girl was dead. The boy was wounded badly, his body covered in blood, his face maimed with the crisscross of the bayonet, which bored through his jaws. Only his eyes moved. He was not dead, yet. Somehow he managed to put his friend back in her jade-green summer dress, he had found a needle and thread to fix the tear. He wanted to see her die in dignity. Then he lay himself next to her, waiting for the fire to expunge their shame – *our* shame. He was surprised to see the young soldier who suddenly appeared in front of him: they were of the same age.

"The boy beckoned the soldier to come closer, showing him the calligraphy scroll he held in his hand. The paper had caught on fire but he wouldn't let go. Stupefied, the soldier looked at the boy and the scroll alternately. 'Are you a spy?' he heard himself ask. '*Are you Communist?*' the soldier pressed on. In his head a hornet nest burst open, everything went black before his eyes. A storm raged inside him. His anger petrified him, the same pernicious poison he felt half a year ago when he left the teahouse near the station. That night the soldier saw his personal enemy.

"The soldier raised his rifle. He couldn't bear the sound of bullets but he could finish it all with a single punch into the disfigured head. Suddenly, the boy raised his face from the expanding blaze. 'Butterfly...' the voice escaped his mouth, and he reached out the flaming scroll to the soldier, who panicked, and jumped back. He smashed the gun into the boy's face.

"The soldier was me, Sato-san," I cried to my dead friend.

"At that moment I still looked for an excuse to get away with! *Oh welcome pure-eye'd Faith, white-handed Hope, Thou hovering angel, girt with golden wings...*But there is no justice in killing either by faith or by law. The moment the boy looked me in my eye, I wanted to know who he was. Where did he come from? Why was he there? What was he trying to say when I raised my rifle to take his life? All at once I had the unyielding, pig-headed wish to find out everything about the person I killed. I want to tell someone he knew how he died. I wanted to relieve myself from the unbearable burden of anonymity so I could face myself.

"Because Sato-san, he was very young. The boy was my age!

"*Uso!*

"The only thing I had of him was a shred left of the burnt scroll when I fought a way out of the scorching fire. The only evidence of my crime! I unfolded the charred rice paper to find the little red heart lying in my palm. Before I left home, Sato-san, I visited a temple to consult my fortune. I never told anyone about this. In the dewpond I found a little fish, its heart was beating and beating through the translucent body – which I took as an auspicious sign.

"On the scalded slice of paper, the cinnabar red heart lay surreptitiously: It was made with the red hot lips of a woman.

I decided I wanted to find the woman, sink or swim, Sato-san.'

I buried my friend not far from where he died. I wrapped his body in the sky blue silk curtain I had wrenched from the window as I broke out the hellhole of gasoline fire in Nanking two years earlier. Sato-san came from the seaside Osaka. He had often told of Osakajo, at whose foot he would lie for hours on end as a child, watching the castle of flying towers like a white crane soaring to rootless clouds – he would die a second time to see the sparkling dome of sky of his hometown. I pictured the blue bliss my friend was guided into, while I closed his grave along a rock-strewn path so I knew someone would pass once in a while, and Sato-san wouldn't be all alone. I prayed the yonder world he entered not be one to make sacrifice of others no matter how marvellous the Cause should sound; a world where the sky-god does not teach hate, and whose gift on New Year's Day is a song almost human. And in case I would return one day to visit, I marked the mound of fresh earth with the crimson rain stone Musume-san gave to me. This was the tombstone I erected for each and every one who died of our wanton cruelty. Their faces flashed back to me. Musume-san my first love, Sato-san my good friend, Madame K., the girl in jade-green summer dress, the boy whose brains I knocked out, even my father. Unbearably lucid faces, with horrid, heartfelt details.

The face of Death.

"Ojiisan! Ojiisan! Wake up!"

His eyes shoot open, lost at first. Then he recognises the nurse's tidy voice.

"You were screaming. I thought I'd better have a look," she says, reaching out to tuck him in.

"What time is it?"

"2 o'clock in the morning. Bad dreams?"

"Dreams. I never knew there were good dreams."

"I found this on the floor – "

"Yes, I think it flew away when I fell asleep. *Domo arigato*."

He takes the little piece in his hand. He doesn't t have to see it, he knew what it is. Life, laughter, *home*. Reality is hazy, life is as certain as an empty page in a book. Something ordinary like a blank sheet of paper can become remarkably extraordinary, just like us. The cauldron of hate can become the holy grail of love. There is more than hate among memory's ruins, the power lies in our own hand to change. He has learnt it from *her*. The magic of this charred little piece of paper can bring him back to her –

"*Flew away?* You mean like a butterfly?"

He screws up his gauzy gaze on her, baffled, lost for words.

"It's in your eyes. Your eyes are full of them, enchanters-on-the-wing. She is very beautiful, judging from her lip…I mean her heart. The heart is painted with her lips, am I right? I'm jealous. Who is she?"

"I told you. She is a fairy. She is my wife. Do you mind passing me my book?"

He leans on the arms of the nurse to raise from the bed and pulls a blanket around his shoulders.

"I'm fine. Thanks."

He opens the fan-shape sheets held together with the narrow stretch of sapphire water, and inserts the burnt shred into its place.

"For seventy years I have never stopped loving her. Seventy years long I have been counting the hours when I can touch her lips again," he mutters, his eyes glazed with a taciturn fever, his shy fingers drawing round the cinnabar strawberry shape, almost perfect. An unabashed moan escapes his throat.

"But you tore out a page. Why?" The nurse points at the toothed fringe along the ribbon.

"It was a little painting of her. I gave it to her on the day we parted. She was worried when we meet up again in the future, we would be too old to recognise each other."

"What's the title of your painting?"

"*1944, Une Passion Chinoise.* She is waiting for me to join her in Wuan."

"That is a place?"

"Wuan, on the bend of a river. Wuan: *Forget me not.*"

"Show me on the map tomorrow. Now get back to sleep fast."

The nurse helps him to lie down again before heading out to the doorway. She halts in her track and turns back to look at him.

"I read it somewhere. 'Love is like war; easy to begin but hard to stop.' Love is a battle, we have to fight for it before we know we cared. Sweet dreams, Ojiisan!"

He listens to the heels ticking pleasantly away on the off-white linoleum, until they fade into a blurred end. He is wide awake, pondering her words. Love and war. It is as a soldier that you make love and as a lover that you make war. Life's nuclear ballet, violent, noisy, and silent. *Kaboom!* In love and war, don't seek counsel. Now that it's all over, what did we do yesterday that's worth mentioning? Be kind to your shadows is the best counsel he ever had in his yesterdays. His mind drifts to the end of the war. He called on his former army officer; Cesaru was dying.

"We really lost it! How could everyone have been so sloppy? How could we have lived on like this?" The war veteran said in an offended voice, but his countenance reflected his tragedy more than his anger.

"When I heard our Emperor on the radio, I pulled back the bolt on my rifle and unloaded the bullets. I eased off the pack that I always carried with me and laid the gun on top of it. Would I really have no more use for the firearm I have polished and cared for like a baby? I asked myself. How about *Yamato damashii*, our nation's strength? The end to that too? Never be captured, never break down, never surrender. To be a coward is a disgrace to our family, our country and our Emperor. We were trained to fight to the death. We were expected to die before suffering humiliations and dishonour. We were supposed to show cheer in the teeth of death and prove our willingness to die in honour. *Yamato Damashii*, the Japanese heart. I found out it is but a scam. All the people who died, I realised that they died for a smokescreen. Then we came back to Japan. But life at home didn't wait for us. Life has become impossible. Like everybody else, I assumed a new identity. I became a bookseller. Imagine me being a bookseller!

"In the beginning I often thought of the girl. I didn't dare to sleep, fearing to see her ghost, her jade-green summer clothes that won't stop wailing. I never get married. I took her phantom as my bride. How could one do such things to another human being, I keep asking myself. The truth is we can and we do. You don't have to look far for a bunch of crap to repeat the madness next year. Sometimes choosing life is choosing a more painful death. I wish I had died with her! Maru-san, your name means a magical pill. It also means a full stop. The end. A "zero" so you can start fresh today. Tell me you have a remedy, I beg of you!"

"After Sato-san died," he recalls he answered. He knew there is no magic to heal their wounds except their memory.

"After Sato-san died, I was alone at night, drinking from the little bottles of eau de cologne he left behind to keep myself warm, I thought of killing myself. One bullet, here, then it's over. Peace."

"I sent you to get my revolver but you never returned...Why didn't you? Kill yourself?"

"I thought of you, commander. I remember the day I joined the unit, you said: 'You are absolutely forbidden to die by your own hand. Under no circumstances are you allowed to give up your life voluntarily.' You said: 'Never forget that as a soldier you have no talent for Thinking!' The truth is, I did a lot of thinking during the long, cold hours I spent alone. I came to the conclusion that dying could be an option but the choice is too easy. Suzuki-san, what happened to him?"

"When we came home, we were hailed as heroes. We were hailed as heroes but all they did was keeping us out of the limelight. Everybody is afraid and ashamed of something nobody talks about. Suzuki-san was confused. When we were enlisted soldiers, we were ready to accept any harsh treatment as part of our duty. We were beaten by high-ranking officers, assigned absurdly strenuous tasks, even cut food and drinks. Glorious death made us beam like school kids. We gave a round of applause to suicidal attacks with bayonets. But then one day, you find out it wasn't like that at all. They may see you as a hero, but in your conscience you carry a whole nation's crime! Suzuki-san bought a ticket to the Philippines. He looked for the most outlying of islands. He lived on bananas and coconuts, and once in a while he would kill a local's cow for dinner. Stuff we learned at the School, you know. He stayed in the jungle until he shot himself in 1975. It was in the newspaper, that's how I knew. He let us know that under no circumstances would he surrender. NEVER! Suzuki-san took glorious death quite literally. But the thing is, no-one dies gloriously."

That was Cesaru, who got his name from the most glorious soldier in history.

"Maru-san?" he spoke again after a significant pause. "After you left us, I reported you were dead. If I told you that the café was not just a café, would you believe me?"

"What do you mean exactly?"

"It's a temporary place of the eternal fire."

"You mean like *purgatory*?"

Without an answer, Cesaru beckoned him to come closer. He folded open his tiny, emaciated hand, showing a mysterious square shape with burnt, rough edge.

"When you didn't come back the next day, I went to the café to look for you. You know what's weird though? The place was gone. Neither a trace of cinders nor smoke was left to be found on the spot. It simply disappeared. But I found this. I have kept it all the year so I can give it back to its owner. Read it."

No. 1 Medical Centre of Nanking
Name: Dr. Reigan
Department: Mental Health
Class Code: 8
Pager: 8-8600.

"It's an ID tag!"

"It's *your* ID tag. Reigan and Maru. The two names are written with the same Chinese ideogram! They both mean magical remedy. A "zero". A full stop after a story of lingering pain, and relief from pain. It's up to us whether to let go or not. What I mean to say is. In another, parallel reality you have made it to become a medical doctor! Go on. Keep it. You will need it pretty soon. *Trust me.*'

"…another, parallel reality?"

"Being a bookseller, I have spent some time digging my nose into Einstein. Popular stuff, no big deal. I'm too thick for hard science. I have to say, the invention of the quantastic space, a place where noises would faint, where people don't stop for lunch, a place that anything at all may happen, with the option to become a time-traveller! I would want to return to Nanking on that day to find the girl and say sorry…" His throat bobbing, his voice dwindled to a sob, wiry brows trembling painfully. Cesaru didn't notice he said quant*a*stic in place of quant*i*stic. Perhaps imagination is the final cure for what makes us suffer.

"I believe you are the one who would understand, Maru-san. You were the only soldier I knew who carried books around. When we were in China fighting our wars, it was you who always found time to read us a story between two bombshells. Your favourite story tells about a man who dreamed of a butterfly, and when he woke, he asked himself whether it was him who dreamed he was a butterfly or a butterfly dreaming of being a human. You would bookmark the story with an empty sheet just so you could find it easily. Every time you took out the sheet, I wondered if our life can ever be the same again, clean, unmarked. The true innocence, like a puppy chasing after a butterfly. They say death is a gateway – "

"I suppose we will see each other again on the other side. Walk onward, children. The past teaches the true friendships along the path of pain and torment."

"If you don't mind my asking, Maru-san. After you disappeared, where did you go? What have you done?"

"I went to chase butterflies in the hills."

"Of course you did. The delicate wings that are yet capable of carrying us from the prison of darkness to the tower of hope – " The dim eyes flared, dismal glints.

"I figured it was the only thing I could do to redeem myself. The only thing I could do to make up for the wrongs."

"I was once like you, Maru-san. Determined, full of purposes. Life makes you do things. In the end, life comes between you and the man you wanted to be."

"Life is old and young every day. I didn't want to be owned by shame like people by their mortgage loans. We can be released of all our chains and make our own future."

"This is the difference between life and fiction: Fiction has to make sense. Did you find any…butterflies?"

"It took me some years, drifting from place to place, using all the tricks of a true bloodhound. Most of the time I was a tongueless beggar. Being neighbour to rats you soon will find the valuables because no-one keeps secrets from rats, do they. Eventually, I found the one I was looking for."

"One butterfly, huh?" the wiry brows shot up. "Did it work?"

"Yes, the only one. It worked."

He stood up to say goodbye.

A few months later he read in obituary section of the newspaper that Cesaru passed away at his home. In his hands he was holding a volume of lepidopterology, an encyclopaedic field guide of rarefied butterflies and moths from all over the world.

In a weird and wonderful little room somewhere on the planet Earth, Dr. Reigan is helping his patient to dust down her memory.

"Run!" she said almost shouting it out at him, gripping his arm.

Startled by the sound of her voice, electrified, Reigan examines her face. He likes it the way he found it, timeless, everlasting. Yet indiscernibly, her features have begun to acquire the hints of age and decay. The slight crow's feet are showing around the eyes, the tiny sagging of the cheeks reveals gradually the triumph of gravity. She looks vulnerable and beautiful, more a woman than a fish. Even her feet are separated now, and between them a seductive line became visible, growing all along her lacy fantail to become her legs. She is too unreal and yet real as real can be. She is granted the power to DIE.

A thousand miles away, in Tokyo, a ninety-year-old man walks the pavement along the Aoyama-dori boulevard. *"Run!"* he hears the voice, as he plots a course across the street flooded with downtown traffic. He halts, in awe of the immense stretch of water swaying from his feet to the horizon. *Shalalala.* He is at the heart of the ocean, looking at it but still understanding nothing of it. Mare Nostrum. Our memories of sleepwalking typhoons and the shipwrecks of love. *Our heart.* He holds his hands afloat and kicks his legs, lured by the voice calling from the depths of time. Fields of green. Looming, blue waves crashing down. The sound of the dream machine. *Shalalala.*

In a weird and wonderful little room somewhere on the planet Earth, Dr. Reigan is helping his patient to dust down her memory.

"You discovered that your young lover was murderer of your son," – Reigan picks up the storyline right where she left off last time – "you decided not to kill him."

"I decided to love him. I decided I would accept him for everything he was. I learned to forgive and how to forgive. The world happens, we can choose how much it happens. At the end of the day no-one loses or wins. There is no future living in the past. For all I know, we could start finding peace and happiness between two human beings. To love, to be loved is the true gift of our heart. Love is not mediocre. Love is our freedom."

"You were pregnant by a man-killer, didn't that bother you?"

"What atonement is there for blood spilt upon the earth! The child was dead before it saw first sun."

She closes her huge eyes.

A thousand miles away, in Tokyo, a ninety-year-old man arrives at the Narita International Airport. People halt their hurried pace. It's a memorable sight, a tantalising spectacle how the old man proceeds to the gate. The airy, tinselled gait as if his soul has fled his body. As if he is pulled forwards by invisible sails. Later on people would recall a radiant nimbus they saw, like an alien sun passing above the

Earth's surface. They saw a flock of stars, the rippling shape of a tail. *Or were they not wings?*

A thousand miles back, in the sickroom, Dr. Reigan asks:

"You lost your child. How?"

"They drowned me. They drowned the adulteress and her lover together."

"That can't be. You must not forget you are a goldfish!"

"So, before what was going to happen next, I wrote one word. I told him: 'Run!' "

"That's the way you parted seventy years ago? He ran?"

A thousand miles away, on JAL flight 321 from Tokyo to China, the ninety-year-old man takes a sip from the drink served around by the cabin attendant. He spills on his clothes. He feels his heart beat faster and faster, thumping everywhere along him so tense and maddening that he is afraid it would fail or burst. He takes another sip of the drink to keep himself calm, ruminating the day seventy years ago.

"Run!" She wrote the single word at the table where he always sat waiting for her. He was not taken by surprise or left to guess. Love as strong as theirs, there should be no fear or doubt. He knew it all along and had prepared for this hour to come. He knew it since the day he discovered that the revolver had disappeared from the shed. Someone stole it.

He never told her before that a man had followed her all the way through the woods to the abandoned house. Her husband was wondering what had happened to his music records. He was not sure what his wife was doing, what the crazy woman was up to. He wanted to know the truth. The voyeur spied on them, first from a distance, his prying face flashing behind the trees. One day, he decided to come closer.

Her husband didn't break in on the lovers. He observed them silently through a narrow slit in the shutters. Soon afterwards he brought along the Chows. The couple had complained that Mr. Fu didn't send them food for a long time. Then, Mr. Fu, her husband laughed with his tough belly, turning the revolver on one finger: "What do we do?" After a quick counsel they swung to action. "Put the gun away, Mr. Fu," Mrs. Chow concluded in a chilly voice. "We MUST obey tradition. We must do our duties," answered the men in choir.

"Run!" she wrote at the table where he always sat waiting for her. He knew it all along and had prepared for this hour to come.

He took to his heels and ran. Who knows what other charges will be filed against him?

"This is what you are telling me?! The soldier spooked and turned tail without even saying goodbye?" In a weird and wonderful little room, Dr. Reigan asks, annoyed, feeling betrayed by how everything turned out. "I must be high. But this is supposed to be a love story! The guy just broke the rules!"

"I'm afraid that's all I have to offer. Broken rules, disenchanted hearts."

"Then your husband and his accomplices came in and found the enemy was gone. Now WHAT?"

"They came in to find me waiting for them. I had changed, and dressed myself in the golden kimono. I had never felt so frightened before. I hugged myself, trying to calm down. Then I walked to the door, led by three people who loathed and hated me more than anything in the world. That was the last time I saw myself in human shape."

"How? What happened?"

"During the summer I consulted local mythology. The diviner I visited told me that physical transformation may be accompanied by a mental transformation, more so if it's involuntary. The witch said it is extremely dangerous since the process can be permanent. It can be irreversible. I believe from that moment on my mind was shutting out to protect me. I have a gap in my memory of what happened. When I came round, I was bleeding."

The man on JAL flight 321 takes a long swig from his drink, down down down down. He recalls the moment he fled the house, and what he did next.

After taking a deep dive in the lotus pond, he buttered his face and shoulders with black mud from the bottom. Under the giant, inky leaves he went, his feet searching in the slushpit, finding a taut knot of roots to step on. He knew every corner of the pond, it was a well-chosen spot where he planted himself.

He waited, holding his impulse in check. The three figures appeared from the house, carrying in their arms a large bundle wrapped in the shining piece of silk. He watched them adding stones to the tied up body. Floating for a moment, the body sank away among the weightless pink and red of flowers, and disappeared. But just as he was about to lose his mind, he saw a small circle of light rising from the invisible depth. A golden bell escaping towards the black water surface, expanding. The radiant glow became a diffuse red, before it scattered to small dust particles, dispersing, vanishing into thin air.

The three figures didn't leave straight away. They walked around the house, searching for the fugitive. Finally at sundown, he sailed out to find her body.

He pulled her out of the water and sealed his month to hers, his hands pumping on the dead heart. A crimson ribbon crept from the mouth corner. He bent to kiss the little spot: it was the sweetest place. He scooped her limp body in his arms. He carried her over the hills. From there he wanted to walk to the dim horizon. He wanted to walk on forever, carrying sun on his shoulders and clutching her body to his chest, without stopping – until the world ends in another new day.

The cold damp wind blew his breath back into his nostrils, crying like a mourning Shakuhachi flute. He choked on a lung-catching gulp of air. Nearby the river flowed forward, foaming ferociously in the bend, tumbling on without looking back.

He tripped, stepping on a sharp rock under the night sky, breaking into a run on the steep side of the hill. From the top, little soundless stones started bouncing down while the larger ones followed more sedately. Before he knew the whole hillside began to slide. A deluge of rocks and earth rolling and shifting on the bare slope, taking the two of them down an endless furrowed path. They hurried over an uncertain edge, and fell into the brawling void of torrents. A violent current swung them against slippery boulders shaped like floating, giant heads on curved, irregular water that glinted red, rushing away between her legs like a broken jar of wine. He held onto her as they went down the womb of darkness, drawn by magnetic swirls of liquid. He wanted to play sailboat with her for the last time. He bent to her, rocking her on inky waves, loving every inch of her skin cold between his lips. The roaring river swelled and rose to a thunder. On the white crest of wave he sang for her: *Summertime...fish are jumpin'...*

Quietly, almost unobserved, like some organism from the deep ocean that only blooms at night, the golden silk unfurled around the pale oval of her face, stunningly beautiful, fading. But then, in the blink of an eye, he saw, just like that, he saw from unintelligible depths a speckled light rising to him. A ginger moon, augmenting, throwing patches of flaked shadows over her milky skin re-emerging. A green bluish light rose from blackness, with a soft, dark pink sheen that made his heart lift. She heard the black velvet voice calling her, and opened her huge eyes in water –

"I opened my eyes in water," Dr. Reigan hears the magical voice filling the weird and wonderful little room, powerful and weak at the same time. *She is dying.*

"I opened my eyes and smiled at him!"

"…"

"Pulled along by the Yangtze's strong waves, feeling the delicious rush, feeling the fishes swimming between our legs, we talked at length."

"…"

"I didn't know before that one could communicate feelings without words, perhaps much deeper feelings. And we made a promise to each other. We decided that we shall part at the point where the Yangtze ends and the sea begins. We shall travel further, alone, each in the opposite direction of the other – "

" 'We shall travel further, alone, each in the opposite direction of the other,' " somewhere in the sky, the man on JAL flight 321 repeats silently the words spoken seven decades ago, " 'until both of us have covered half circle round the Earth to meet up again. That will be the day our world has changed and not be the same one where we once loved and cared despite the horror that surrounded us.' "

"How do we find each other?" asked the shiny body swimming close to his.

" 'How do we find each other,' I asked, keeping close to him, afraid that the river would end too soon and separate us too early."

In the weird and wonderful little room, Reigan listens to the voice recounting an astonishing promise made seven decades ago by two swimmers in the Yangtze.

" 'Spring Green, Wisconsin,' he said."

Above the Chinese sea, the man on JAL flight 321 looks to the iceberg clouds outside the window. He recalls the night seven decade ago. Drifting alongside her, not losing her lustrous, slender body like a beacon in dark water, he hung on as long as he could. To see them from afar they would be no more than two dots or two playing dolphins for the more imaginary eyes.

"Taliesin," he said.

"In the lush green of Wisconsin, there is a house on the shining brow near the waterfall," Dr. Reigan listens to the account of a journey plotting through all its twists and turns to find an end as it should be.

"I remember the picture he showed me. The house looked exactly like the place I found a home in the summer nearly seventy years ago. We even painted the black-and-white picture, we painted the roof in faded crimson. 'Taliesin means radiant brow,' he said to me. 'Ever since I was a kid, I have dreamed to live there with someone I love – in a pink-roofed house,' he said to me."

" '*É meu e vosso este fado destino que nos amarra...*' " Over the mountains, the man on JAL flight 321 hums to himself, like he sang for her decades ago:

" *'This fate is mine and yours, destiny that keeps us tied…'* "

" *'Esta tristeza que trago Foi de vós que a recebi…'* " Reigan hears the fantastic creature sing to herself, stunned by the sight of the glittering little pieces of sequins on her arms and covering the small of her back. The scales are disappearing! Her skin is peeling, picking up a pale sheen so lucent he could map the veins like infinitesimal rivers on a ramshackle wonderland of the past!

"I'm such a poor singer," she smiles shyly. "I remember every note he sang for me in the summer before the war ended. *This fate is mine and yours, destiny that keeps us tied, the sadness inside me, it came from thy…*"

"Why didn't you travel to Taliesin, Wisconsin to meet him?" Dr. Reigan persisted, knowing she could die any moment.

"One war ended. The other began. War followed by war. When peace came, China was closed to the outside world."

"But you could set out and leave. YOU could, by swimming across the ocean. You promised him *'no matter what'*, didn't you?"

"When I looked in the mirror, I saw an old woman. Missing made me age. Don't you know, Doctor? Goldfish are like swans, they mate for life. If one is gone, the other loses its shine and dies in the end."

"You shall not die alone, I swear," the man whispers to the brilliant sun shining through clouds. "I have come to sing you a song so you don't die in silence. *No matter what.*" He whispers to his memory.

They are landing. His eyes searching the hilly landscape he recognises, suddenly he feels anxious. *What if it's not there, not anymore?* Then, in his tear-blurred vision – or it was his mind's eye? – he captures, among the enclosing green where the grave, earthen brow skews at a sharp angle into the bent water, the soupcon the size of a rekindled gem, frightening but important – almost like a talisman from the past, like faith's faithless pattern: a pink shadow floating on a wave of silent whistle. *Shalalala*.

His unease sharpens. What if she asks why it took you so long where have you been I was afraid I'm going to die without seeing you again. He would tell her that he kept his promise. He had been to Taliesin, the other pink-roofed home on the other end of the world where he waited for her. He waited until waiting became his life. One morning when he woke up, he went to pack. He travelled further north along the coast, which took him to the violet woodlands where he received blessings from the medicine man. Then he left the solid land behind him. He finished the other half circle of the Earth she never made and came at last to the closed borders of the country. Having no choice, he made the ocean crossing back home. For the first time since he didn't remember when, he set foot on his native soil where he waited more, and whenever he felt he was losing heart, he would take out the charred little piece of paper to remember. The summer of 1944 would flood back to his memory, a golden, eternal sea: he did not allow the fire in his heart to burn out – even though seared chicken heart isn't particularly his favourite dish at the local Yakitori restaurant. And then, as he walked up the Aoyama-dori boulevard one day, he heard her calling from the murmuring seas of pain…and *tenderness*. The tenderness of a good Takoyaki dish, grilled fresh pink to go with tempura scraps, pickled ginger, and green onion. An excellent chef would spend hours to massage the octopus. Death needs a good squeeze of a pair of kind, caring hands to become sweet and succulent. That's the right way to do it, the only way: to die feeling her hands on his body, her tender, loving fingers grill him, fry him on fire. The time has come at last. The river is calling for the fishes to come home for a banquet of love! A song of songs!

In the weird and wonderful little room somewhere on the planet Earth, Dr. Reigan suddenly yells:

"What the hell is going on?"

He holds himself taut against his chair, seeking to balance on a sudden release of energy shattering the ground under his feet. The seismic waves creases the shell of the floor, tearing it open, baring layers of naked crust. He is tipped back by a series of tremor. A few inches above his head he feels a huge shadow of metallic shine zooming past.

"Is this how it's going to end, with crashing flying machine?" he shouts, his voice lost in deafening noises.

"The UFO has landed, Doctor," she answers in a voice lucid as a dream. "If you open the door, you will find a man there. Don't be afraid, he may look a little strange. Let him in. Go on."

Reigan can't quite believe what he sees. The man's face is gigantic yet small, wrinkly yet young. Numerous tendrils of hair bouncing on his head – numerous rivers singing a song of sadness and happiness.

The man stretches out his hand. He clips the name tag back on the cord hung from Reigan's neck. Reigan watches the burnt edge restore to a perfect square. Somewhere, sometime he must have lost his ID. He didn't notice that the cord was empty.

The ear-splitting sound dies away all of a sudden. Reigan feels a burning sensation inside his head. Hundreds of questions which he is unable to ask, as if he lost his tongue. A small voice trickles from nowhere, fills up the room and becomes legible:

"You are the one who holds the key, Dr. Reigan. The answer has always been there, sitting on your bookshelf, written on the page bookmarked with a blank sheet of paper."

The man unfurls a graceful slow-motion across the room. A river of wounded memory. The radiant water curls up beside her, harbouring her body in his arms like nocturnal waves caressing a little white sailboat in the moon.

"Do not die, do not die, do not die," he sings in her ear the lullaby. Or it was: "Let it go, let it go, let it go."

The song is torn to rags by water jets pushing through the ruptured seams of the floor. Reigan recognises the shape of an ancient well. The liquid surface rushing up to meet him, expunging the last detail of the room.

They are drowning.

Reigan opens his eyes. How long has he been here? His back hurt from unchanged position. He must have fallen asleep just like that, standing, bending over the stretcher cart. He pulls back the white sheet to cover the dead woman's body. Her exceptional physical attractiveness adds an odd, chilling quality to her features. Big lashes skirting the delicate, china-like eyeshells, a vivid mouth, and a pert nose which he can't resist to touch. He lays a finger to the perfect arch, a touch so brief as if only to tap air. He recalls that he was called to the morgue this afternoon to check on a case of brain death. It came a bit out of the blue, but it does happen, and Reigan said he would. A fragment of his dream flashes back to him, like a spell, without as much as a dwindled thought.

It has been a hell of a fortnight. Half of the metropolitan population suffers from heavy migraine, whose cause still remains unidentified. A patient brought in this morning emptied the entire content of his breakfast on him. The other night at home, Alice went on and on about them having a baby.

He picks up the penlight dropped to the floor and heads to the heavy metal entry. *"Funny,"* he thinks, passing the door next to the morgue. The sickroom has been kept empty and locked ever since the war and he never asked why.

Something attracts his attention. The seal on the door is broken, somebody must have entered the room. He reaches out to touch the rusty padlock. There is something strangely prehistoric about the image on the cast iron face. It reminds him of some sort of hybrid of a fish and a butterfly.

He proceeds to the lift and pushes the up button.

"Put on a light for heaven's sake!"

Nurse Lyn walks in with a steaming cup in one hand, her other hand rubbing up and down the wall for a light switch.

"I brought you coffee, Dr. Reigan."

"Sorry, I forgot time passing while walking in the woods and finding some magic mushrooms and berries to pick. Mmmm. Heavenly mud, the slurpier the better."

His eyes batting from the sudden glare of electric light tubes, Reigan takes a big sip, running the hot liquid over his tongue. He hears a faint buzzing in his head. For hours he has been hiding in his office, browsing the Internet, searching for something, anything at all.

"It's ten o'clock. I'm off. Is there something wrong, Dr. Reigan? We haven't seen you since the afternoon."

"Just…some study. A rare medical case I discovered in the history. At least, I'm not sure yet if it's an ailment…To tell the truth, I'm checking Google gallery for a fish called the butterfly fish."

"Any luck?"

"Now I know that butterfly fish don't look like a butterfly at all. It's…"

"It's a goldfish," the nurse cuts in affirmatively. "A girl from the nursing school once kept one in our dormitory. Goldfish are very smart. They have keen senses and recognise the footsteps that bring them food. Girls fought to feed the fish, we vied for the honour and competed who found the most delicious flakes.'

"Why the name?"

"They say butterfly fish was made by Bodhisattva Guan Yin after she had a strange dream. Guan Yin looked at the star-studded body hauling a fantail so black like ink spilled in water. At that moment a butterfly floated past her. One thing other fish don't do, though. A real butterfly fish can change into a beautiful woman at night."

"Did it?"

"It died. The girl told us that in order to achieve the metamorphosis, people need to focus their mind, to such an extent that you feel the intense boiling pain in your skull."

"You mean like a migraine attack? *Why?*"

"Surely you know, Dr. Reigan. Before the attack begins, the patient undergoes extreme sensory stimuli. Many of them can see a strange light, tints of bright golden yellow, kinda looks like Hiroshima swallowing you up. If a large number of people see that light at once, chances are the magic fish will turn into a real woman. Damn, I'm late. There is a dance party.

My girlfriend is waiting for me on the Bund. See you tomorrow, Dr. Reigan."

The nurse turns to leave with a smile.

"Thanks for coffee, Lyn! Kick up your heels!" Reigan calls after her, listening to her heels ticking pleasantly away on the off-white linoleum. The sleek red shine of leather dissolves all the way up to the bend in the corridor. The shoes remind him of the word "desire".

Stretching skywards then rubbing his eyes, he takes off his jacket. It's time to go home. Heading up to the lift, he passes the room around the corner. Nurse Lyn forgot to close the window. Walking to the view, he leans out over the ledge to feel the first rain in his face. He breathes in the cooling breeze. It's over. The lightning cracks the black sky, bringing along a series of rolling sounds. Heartland thunders, the giant inky leaves chant in choir. He pulls down the storm shutter and secures the latches and bolts. Suddenly, he narrows his eyes, staring into the fishbowl in the windowsill. Wonderstruck, he watches the black satin tail opens like a tender blossom, the lengthening filaments revealing a new layer that slowly unfolds itself. *There are two of them!* He discovers a tiny, blushing spot hidden in the corner of the mouth, not too high and not too low, not too big and not too small. An imperfection exactly right. The glittery gingery bodies chase after each other into the unbound space, two pairs of wings twirling like spilled satin in water.

Reigan straightens to hunt in his pocket for the cell phone and dials Alice's number.

"The typhoon is coming." He pauses as if to catch breath. "I love you, sweetheart. Let's make babies. Lots of babies, like fishes do."

He closes the phone and switches off the light. In his wake something lifts from the tabletop on a shadow of stirred air, flitting. An untethered flower propelling in the dark to kiss the sun of tomorrow and find the shoulders to light on to bring them luck, happiness and riches beyond time and place. The charred edge scintillating like a radiant smile, showing the cinnabar red shade of a heart on its aged surface.

THE END

Keynote from the author:

To write this book, I drew inspiration from an ancient Chinese story I read when I was a child:

Zhuangzi dreamed he was a butterfly, flitting around in the sky; then he awoke. Now he wonders: Am I a man who dreamt of being a butterfly, or am I a butterfly dreaming that I am a man.

A tale from the 4th century BC

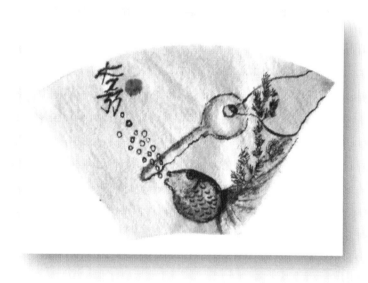

This is a work of fiction. A few liberties have been taken with the historical record in the interests of the truth.

An astonishing story of Linden, Kai and Lana, their hellish love triangle in the summer of 1989, shortly before the 4 June Massacre took place on the Tiananmen Square in Beijing. Twenty years later, Linden wakes up one morning to find Kai, carrying his cello, at the doorstep of her apartment in a North-European city. Obviously, her childhood love has hunted her down. As Kai enters her life again, together they open a hidden door in her wardrobe; the secret entrance leads to their heart. They peer into their shared past where there is a secret garden, "the smallest and most intimate of gardens". The mystery around Lana's death slowly drops veil...

China Sonata on Amazon Kindle
autumn 2012

Made in the USA
Lexington, KY
22 February 2012